# COOKING
## salmon & steelhead

Exotic recipes from
around the world

## Scott & Tiffany Haugen

**Frank Amato**
**PORTLAND**

# Acknowledgments

We would like to thank all of the people who lent a helping hand in the creation of this book. From those who generously offered their favorite family recipe, to the Indonesian market worker who unknowingly educated us on so many of the world's spices. It's people like you who allowed this book to take on a unique flavor.

Though many recipes within these pages are our original ideas, tried and tested in our home over many years, we still credit several people with at least a part of them. Having the chance to travel the world taught us about cooking on a level we never before considered, adding variety and pleasure to our daily lives and our diet. For this we are in deep appreciation to all the friendly folks who opened our eyes to cooking made simple, on a global scale.

Published in 2003 by
Frank Amato Publications, Inc.
PO Box 82112 • Portland, Oregon 97282 • (503) 653-8108
Softbound ISBN: 1-57188-291-X • Softbound UPC: 0-81127-00120-0
Photography by Scott Haugen
Book Design: Esther Poleo
Printed in Singapore

# Contents

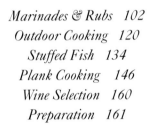

# Dedication

*T*his book is dedicated to Jerry and Jean Haugen. The continual assistance and support you provided during the creation of this work means more to us than you'll ever know. Always lending a helping hand when needed, be it catching fish, cleaning up the kitchen or most importantly, tending to your two grandsons, allowed us to stay focused and see this project to the end. Without you, it wouldn't have happened.

It is our ultimate desire to be parents as supportive as you are; always there for our children when they need us. If every child and grandchild had the influence of people like you in their lives, the world would be a better place. Thank you and God bless.

*Scott & Tiffany Haugen*

# Introduction

The array of cookbooks on the market can be overwhelming, but few titles are solely dedicated to the cooking of salmon and steelhead. Of those that do relate to preparing these fish, certain ingredients and complicated handling processes make creating some of the recipes impractical for a large percentage of people.

The primary goal of this book is to offer tasty recipes that are easy to follow with ingredients conveniently attained at the local grocery store. At the same time, we have included a selection of indulgent recipes, any of which the average home cook can create.

Since the late 1800s, our relatives have been catching and cooking salmon and steelhead in Oregon's Willamette Valley. Once we married and moved to Alaska — where we spent most of the 1990s — we adopted a subsistence lifestyle. Nearly every meal centered around the game and fish we harvested from the land.

Though we lived in the Alaskan Arctic, we spent a few days each summer on the Kenai Peninsula, catching and storing salmon for shipment into the small Eskimo village we called home. In this isolated village setting, cooking ingredients were minimal, and we bought all we needed while passing through the cities of Anchorage or Fairbanks, once a year.

While some excellent recipes in this book have been shared by chefs, restaurants and private individuals, the majority stem from Tiffany's creative mind, a result of all the time she's spent in the kitchen over the years. Raising two boys of our own, we eat fish several times a week in our household, and Tiffany is always originating new and exciting ways to prepare these meals.

Our worldly travels have also impacted the contents of this book. We've been fortunate enough to have visited nearly 30 countries, and tasted very distinct dishes from many of them. Stemming from our global experiences, we've assembled a collection of dishes exemplifying the unique tastes from the many countries we visited. In capturing these special cultural blends, we've gone to the effort of including ingredients that can be easily attained, no matter where you live.

*Pursuing salmon and steelhead is one of the fishing world's greatest thrills.*

This book is designed to serve the needs of people looking to diversify their salmon and steelhead recipes; the ones who have one or two favorites they stick to, no matter how many fish may be stashed in the freezer. It's also geared to those who head to the market and purchase a fillet to cook on special occasions. No matter how much fish you cook, the recipes found in this book will greatly expand your options.

From a nutritional perspective, salmon and steelhead are an excellent source of quality protein, essential amino acids, vitamins and minerals. The fats contained in these wild fish are largely unsaturated and noted for their help in preventing coronary heart disease. In addition to carrying fat-soluble vitamins, fish also contains water-soluble vitamins, something the human body processes quickly and requires daily. Some vitamins and minerals found in fish include but are not limited to vitamins A, $B_3$, $B_6$, $B_{12}$, D, E, thiamin ($B_1$), riboflavin ($B_2$), calcium, iron, magnesium, niacin, potassium, phosphorous and zinc. In addition, fish is very low in cholesterol. The belly, collar and dark meat of fish are where the highest oil and mineral contents are found.

Present-day science accepts that the type of dietary fat we consume modifies the production of biological compounds called eicosanoids. It's thought these compounds aid in blood clotting, regulating blood pressure, proper functioning of the immune system, controlling inflammation and rheumatoid arthritis. It's been shown that the omega-3 oils, a polyunsaturated fat component in fish, produce eicosanoids, which further minimize the risk of heart disease, inflammation and some cancers. Scientific studies have also suggested that omega-3 oils noticeably reduce stress, depression and bipolar disorders, and may also aid in infant brain and retinal development. Recent studies have even put fish oils in a category with other healthy oils and stated our bodies burn these fats more efficiently, thus reducing excess fat absorption. Salmon, considered a fatty fish, has one of the highest counts of omega-3s, with up to 100 times the levels found in other meats such as beef, lamb or poultry.

When it comes to specific recipes in this book, we will not differentiate between the five Pacific salmon species, other world salmon or winter and summer steelhead. Though from a nutritional perspective, wild fish have more to offer than farm-raised fish, for all intensive purposes we will refer to both salmon and steelhead, be they wild or farmed, as "fish" from this point on.

So much of what goes into a fish before it winds up on the platter can have a major impact on its overall flavor. Proper caring for a fish, from the time it's caught to the time of preparation, has a tremendous influence on the taste of the end product. Personal preference also plays a part. For example, some people refuse to eat fall-run chinook due to their high oil content. Others will only eat fall-run chinook due to the their high oil content. Many folks prefer red salmon over all other species, while some prefer chinook and coho to the reds.

Then there's the consideration of where a fish comes from. We'll eat an

*In addition to essential vitamins and minerals, salmon contains one of the highest counts of omega-3 oils of any meat. Preparing your own fish means you don't have to depend on commercial supplements.*

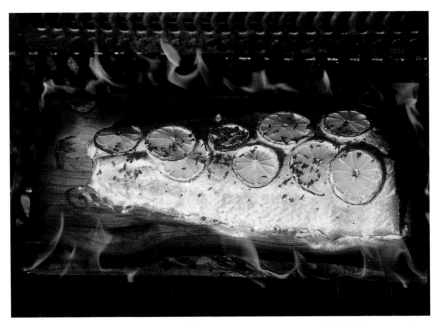

*Plank cooking your fish is just one of the numerous ways to prepare a delightful, hearty meal.*

ocean- going chum or pink salmon any time, but once they've hung in a river for an extended period, eating them is the farthest thing from the mind. Some individuals are so selective when it comes to eating fish, noting differences in oil content, meat color and texture from different river systems, that they may only dine on fish taken from specific drainages. Some folks may only eat fish taken from a specific river during the month of May, leaving the same species alone during June, claiming warming water temperatures and increased slime production impact the quality of the meat.

In other words, there are many beliefs surrounding the point of which fish species tastes best. This is another reason this cookbook was created; to offer a variety of recipes and flavors that appeal to each individual, for not all of us share the same tastes.

Keep in mind, a recipe is only as complicated as you make it. There are many shortcuts that can be taken if under time constraints or if lacking certain ingredients. By having ingredients on-hand, prior to deciding to cook a certain recipe, the effort becomes easier and more enjoyable. There are other steps that can be taken to simplify the cooking process, should you feel so inclined. For instance, dried herbs can be substituted for many of the fresh herbs in the recipes. No doubt, fresh herbs offer a fuller flavor over dried, but the dishes will still retain their distinct flavors. Many prepared items can also be substituted, such as minced garlic from a jar instead of fresh cloves, or lime juice from a bottle versus fresh-squeezed. Some people may balk at even the thought of introducing diced tomatoes from a can, but leave the options open. When there are toddlers tugging at your pant legs in the kitchen or you're scrambling to prepare a meal on a tight timeline, corners can be cut in many cases.

When cooking any of the recipes within these pages, keep in mind that experimentation is welcome. Don't forego a recipe simply because you may not have canola oil; substitute olive oil or butter instead. If on a restricted diet, omit the salt in the recipes, or apply a butter substitute rather than the real thing. You will still have a delicious meal to serve at the table.

# Appetizers

Appetizers can be one of the most important elements at a dinner party, often setting the tone for the entire evening. As you'll discover after creating some of the following recipes, the only drawback is that appetizers often disappear quicker than planned. While cooked fish can be used in most of these recipes, we prefer smoked fish in many of them for the distinct flavor it provides. The popularity of these tiny treats offer unique tastes accenting other foods, and opportunities to create impressive spreads. Served in large or small portions, appetizers present many wonderful options.

# Sushi Rolls

*Following an enlightening Make Your Own Sushi party at the home of good friends Steve and Joy Davey, we were thrilled to learn that making California rolls is easy and enjoyable. Popular at any gathering, these appetizers are unique and habit forming.*

- **4 cups cooked white, medium-grain rice**
- **1/2 cup rice vinegar**
- **4 tablespoons sugar**
- **2 teaspoons salt**
- **1 package nori (roasted seaweed)**
- **2 cups smoked salmon**
- **3 carrots**
- **1 red pepper**
- **1 cucumber**
- **1 bunch fresh cilantro**
- **2 avocados (omit if not serving immediately)**
- **Sesame seeds**
- **Wasabi paste**
- **Soy sauce**
- **Rice vinegar**
- **Bamboo mat**

Have ingredients ready to go into the rolls before the rice is finished cooking. Work fish into large bite-sized pieces, certain all bones are removed, and set aside. Cut all vegetables in long narrow strips. Steam or microwave carrots and red pepper for a few minutes in the microwave so they are tender; steam them in a splash of rice vinegar for added flavor. Wash and pick leaves off cilantro. Mix vinegar, sugar and salt and set aside. The next step is best with two people. As soon as rice is cooked, transfer into a casserole dish. Pour vinegar mixture over rice and immediately begin to gently stir together. While one person is stirring the rice mixture, another person needs to be fanning the rice. This cools the rice quickly while the vinegar soaks in and also makes the rice nice and shiny. Mix until there is no remaining liquid, no more than 2 minutes. Cover rice with damp towel.

Lay a nori wrapper on the bamboo mat. Slightly wet hands and scoop approximately 2/3 cup of rice, spreading in a thin layer on the nori. Add vegetables, smoked salmon, cilantro and sprinkle sesame seeds if desired. Roll up nori gently, but firmly, and squeeze down on the bamboo mat to shape the roll. Shape as desired in a circle, square or triangle. Unroll the mat and place the roll on a cutting surface. Using a very sharp, damp knife, cut into desired portions 1/2" to 1" thick. Serve with wasabi and soy sauce for dipping.

*These bite-sized treats travel well and make a bright addition to any hors d'oeuvres platter or potluck*

Rinse cherry tomatoes and pat dry. Cut off top 1/4 of tomatoes scooping out seeds and flesh with a small spoon or paring knife. Lay upside down on a paper towel to drain while preparing the filling. Work fish into tiny flakes, certain all bones are removed.

Mix cream cheese, lemon juice and Worcestershire sauce until smooth. Add chopped herbs and mix thoroughly. Stir in flaked, smoked fish and spoon mixture into a cake decorating/frosting bag. Immediately pipe salmon mixture into cherry tomatoes. Cover and refrigerate 30 minutes to 6 hours.

- 25-30 cherry tomatoes, 2 pints
- 1 1/2 cups flaked, smoked salmon or steelhead
- 1 8-ounce package cream cheese (at room temperature)
- 1 tablespoon lemon juice
- 1 teaspoon Worcestershire sauce
- 1 tablespoon fresh parsley, finely minced
- 1 tablespoon fresh basil, finely minced
- 1/2 tablespoon fresh mint, finely minced

# Hot Smoky Dip

*Wonderful with tortilla chips or slices of French baguette, this dip is always the first to go at any gathering.*

- 1 1/2 cups flaked smoked salmon or steelhead
- 1 cup mayonnaise
- 1 cup parmesan cheese
- 1 6 ounce can black olives, sliced
- 1 4 ounce can fire roasted mild green chilies, diced
- 1 cup Monterey jack cheese
- 1/2 cup cheddar cheese

Work fish into small flakes, certain all bones are removed, set aside. Mix remaining ingredients, reserving 1/2 cup parmesan cheese for the top of dip. Gently fold smoked salmon into the mayonnaise and cheese mixture. Spread into a 9" by 12" glass casserole dish, or divide into oven-proof serving dishes of choice and top with remaining parmesan cheese. Bake in a preheated oven at 400° for 25 minutes. Cool 5-10 minutes before serving.

# Tomato Basil Bruschetta

*The aroma alone of this appetizer will have everyone
crowding to the kitchen, ready for a treat.*

Work fish into tiny flakes, certain all bones are removed, set aside. In a small bowl, gently mix tomatoes, basil and pine nuts. Cut baguette into 1/2" slices. Peel the garlic and rub firmly on each side of the baguette slices. Brush both sides of each slice of baguette with olive oil. Place on oven-safe rack, and put tomato mixture on each slice of bread. Place salmon evenly on each piece around the tomato mixture. Broil on high for 1-3 minutes, watching closely. The bruschetta is done when the pine nuts and baguette are golden brown. The bruschetta can also be toasted on an outside grill.

- 1/2 cup cooked, flaked salmon or steelhead
- 1/2 cup diced tomatoes
- 1/4 cup fresh basil, chopped finely
- 1/3 cup pine nuts
- 3 cloves whole garlic
  Olive oil
- 1 baguette, a firm loaf of bread works best

# Smokey Garlic Cheese Bread

*Served with soup or a salad, this crunchy flavorful
bread accentuates any meal.*

- 1 loaf French bread
- 1 cup smoked salmon
- 1/2 cup butter at
  room temperature
- 1/2 cup mayonnaise
- 3/4 cup parmesan cheese
- 4 tablespoons
  minced garlic
- 2/3 cup green onions,
  thinly sliced

Slice French bread lengthwise, set aside. Work fish into small flakes, certain all bones are removed, set aside. Cream the butter and mayonnaise in a medium bowl. Blend in fish, parmesan cheese and garlic. Spread mixture on each half of bread. Top each side with green onions. Broil on low for 3-6 minutes, or until top is lightly browned. Slice and serve hot.

# Creamy Lox & Dill Dip

*This versatile dip goes well with bread, raw veggies and most chips. It can even be used as a salad dressing.*

Mix cream cheese, mayonnaise, whipped cream, milk and lemon juice in a food processor until fluffy. Gently fold in herbed gravlax and chives. Garnish with additional chopped, fresh chives. Serve with bread, raw vegetables or as a chip dip.

- 1/3 cup chopped herbed gravlax (see index for gravlax recipe)
- 4 ounces cream cheese, softened
- 2 tablespoons mayonnaise
- 1 tablespoon whipped cream
- 2 tablespoons milk
- 1 tablespoon lemon juice
- 1 tablespoon fresh chives, finely chopped

# Tropical Bacon Roll-Ups

*When looking for hors d'oeuvres, these bite-sized appetizers are full of flavor and easy to prepare.*

- 12-16 ounces salmon or steelhead, skinned and deboned
- 1 pound bacon
- 1 20-ounce can pineapple chunks

Cut fish into bite sized chunks, about the same size as a piece of pineapple. Cut bacon strips in half. Wrap a half slice of bacon around one pineapple chunk and one piece of raw salmon. Spear with a toothpick. Place bacon wraps evenly on a broiler pan. Broil on medium heat 3-6 minutes or until bacon is crisp. Serve immediately.

# Lox Bites

*These very simple appetizers offer elegance to any gathering. Smoked salmon can be substituted for the gravlax.*

Cut bread into 1/2" slices. Spread cream cheese evenly over each slice. Cut gravlax into thin strips, roll up and place on top of the cream cheese. If using smoked salmon, flake off a piece to sit atop the cream cheese on bread. Garnish with fresh, chopped chives.

- 3 ounces herbed gravlax or smoked salmon (see index for gravlax recipe)
- 4 ounces cream cheese, softened
- 1 loaf french or sourdough baguette

# Salmon Puffs

*A family Christmas delight, no one was ever late to Grandma's house for fear they would miss out on these favorites.*

PUFFS:
- 1 cup 7-Up
- 1/2 cup butter or margarine
- 1 cup flour
- 4 large eggs

FILLING:
- 1 1/2 cups flaked, cooked or smoked salmon or steelhead
- 1 8-ounce package whipped cream cheese (at room temperature)
- 1/4 teaspoon salt
- 1/4 teaspoon pepper
- 2 tablespoons finely sliced green onion

Bring 7-Up and butter to a boil in a medium saucepan. Add flour, mix until smooth. Remove from heat. Add eggs one at a time and beat after each. Drop mixture, by teaspoonful, on a cookie sheet. Bake in a preheated oven at 350° for about 10 minutes (watch closely). They should be lightly browned on top. Let puffs cool.

Work fish into tiny flakes, certain all bones are removed. Cream fish, salt, pepper, cream cheese and green onion together. Slice puffs in half and stuff with filling. Makes 25-30 puffs. Serve immediately or keep refrigerated.

*With several presentation options, this dip can be made
again and again with guaranteed success.*

Work smoked meat into tiny flakes, certain all bones are removed. Mix cream cheese and sour cream until smooth. Add Worcestershire sauce, garlic powder and onion powder and mix thoroughly. Gently stir in flaked smoked fish and you're set. The dip can be served right away, or cooled in the refrigerator for two hours, shaped into a ball and rolled in crushed almonds or walnuts for a decorative presentation. Refrigerate unused portions for future use.

- 1 1/2 cups flaked, smoked salmon or steelhead
- 1 8-ounce package cream cheese (room temperature)
- 1/2 cup sour cream
- 1 teaspoon Worcestershire sauce
- 1/2 teaspoon garlic powder
- 1/2 teaspoon onion powder

# Easy Dip

*Sharon Weber, home economist authority, shares this favorite recipe, stating the green Tobasco gives it great flavor.*

- 1/2-pint jar of canned, smoked salmon
- 1 tablespoon juice from can of salmon
- 8 ounces cream cheese
- A few dashes of green Tobasco sauce
- Fresh ground black pepper to taste

Mix all ingredients until combined. Serve with Wheat Thins or preferred crackers.

# *Stuffed Mushrooms*

*Easy to prepare in advance and pop in the oven when the time comes, these tasty treats are always a favorite.*

Clean mushrooms and remove stems. Place mushrooms on a greased cookie sheet and set aside. Work fish into tiny flakes, certain all bones are removed, set aside. Melt butter in a medium saucepan on medium-low heat. Sauté onions until translucent, add garlic and lightly sauté. Remove from heat and add bread crumbs, Italian seasoning, fish and parmesan cheese, mixing well. Generously fill mushroom caps with mix, packing it down. Broil on low for 5-7 minutes, watching closely. Garnish with finely chopped tomatoes and fresh basil, if desired.

- 1 cup finely flaked, cooked salmon or steelhead
- 30-35 medium mushrooms
- 1/2 cup butter
- 1/4 cup finely chopped onion
- 2 cloves minced garlic
- 3/4 cup bread crumbs
- 1/2 teaspoon Italian seasoning
- 1/2 cup parmesan cheese

# Fish Fritters

*One of Grandma's most requested meals to accompany shrimp salad. These tasty fritters are quite popular as appetizers as well.*

- 4 cups flaked, cooked salmon or steelhead
- 2 cups white flour
- 2 teaspoons baking powder
- 2 teaspoons salt
- 4 eggs
- 1 cup milk
- 2 teaspoons vegetable oil
- Vegetable oil for frying

Mix dry ingredients in a medium-sized mixing bowl. Make a well in the center and add eggs, milk and vegetable oil. Mix thoroughly by hand until smooth, do not over beat. Work fish into small flakes, certain all bones are removed, set aside. Gently fold fish into batter mixture. Using an electric frying pan, add 1 1/2" of oil to the pan. Heat the oil to 350°. Using a large tablespoon, drop fritters carefully into oil and fry until golden brown on each side, turning once (approximately 2 minutes on each side). Drain on a wire rack or paper towels. Serve hot with dip (mix of 3 parts mayonnaise to 1 part ketchup).

# The Original Sandwich Spread

*One of our favorite sandwiches is made from this spread.*
*Scott grew up eating these sandwiches in his school lunches.*

Work cooked fish into small flakes, ensuring no bones remain. In a separate bowl combine mayonnaise, celery, relish, onion, salt and pepper. Add flaked fish and gently mix. The spread is ready to make into a sandwich or put in a bowl to serve with crackers. Keep unused portions refrigerated until ready to serve.

- 2 cups cooked, flaked salmon or steelhead
- 3/4 cup mayonnaise
- 1/2 cup finely chopped celery
- 1/4 cup sweet pickle relish
- 1/4 cup finely chopped onion (optional)
- 1/2 teaspoon salt
- Dash of black pepper

# Twist of Lemon Pate

*The smoked fish in this recipe combined with the lemon and parsley, makes a zesty pate that can be served before a formal dinner, or taken along on a picnic.*

- 1 cup smoked salmon or steelhead
- 6 ounces cream cheese, softened
- 2 tablespoons mayonnaise
- 3 tablespoons lemon juice
- 1 tablespoon Worcestershire sauce
- 1 tablespoon horseradish
- 1 teaspoon paprika
- 2 tablespoons chopped onion or 1/2 teaspoon onion powder
- 1/3 cup fresh parsley

Work fish into small flakes, certain all bones are removed. Blend all ingredients in food processor. Garnish with fresh parsley. Serve with crackers, toast points or bagel chips.

# Pinwheel Wraps

*A great alternative to a traditional sandwich, wraps travel well and can be stuffed with just about anything. Sliced, they make very attractive, eye-catching appetizers.*

Work fish into small flakes, certain all bones are removed, set aside. Laying the wrap, bread or tortilla flat, spread a 1/4" layer of cream cheese over the entire surface. Starting at one end, lay the flaked, smoked salmon in a one-inch-wide strip. Follow with one leaf of lettuce and a one-inch strip of finely diced vegetables. Roll bread, wrap or tortilla starting at the end with the salmon. Roll it all the way up using the cream cheese to seal the end. Cut in half and serve as a "wrap" or slice in 1/2" to 1" sections for pinwheels. Keep refrigerated until ready to serve. Can be made up to 6-8 hours in advance.

Pate Variation: Use Twist of Lemon Pate (previous recipe) in place of the cream cheese and smoked salmon.

- 6-12 wraps, flatbread or flour tortillas
- 1 8-ounce package cream cheese, softened or whipped
- 1-2 cups smoked salmon, flaked with bones removed
- 6-12 lettuce leaves
- Assorted diced vegetables (red or green bell pepper, carrots, jicama, celery, and/or cucumber)

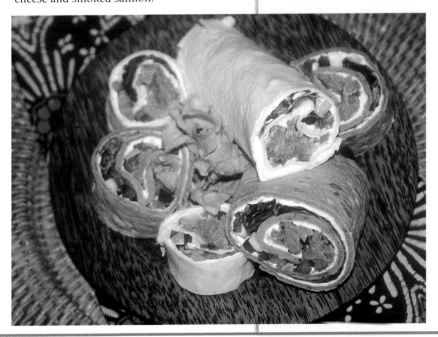

# Fresh Garden Salsa

*A nice way to enjoy all the fresh vegetables of summertime.*
*Fish can also be added to purchased or home-canned salsa.*

- 1 cup cooked, flaked salmon or steelhead
- 2 cups tomatoes, peeled and diced
- 1/2 cup onion, diced
- 1-2 tablespoons jalapeno pepper, diced
- 1 clove garlic, diced
- 1/2 cup green pepper, diced
- 1/2 teaspoon salt
- 1/4 teaspoon cumin
- 2 teaspoons sugar
- 1 tablespoon lemon juice
- 3 tablespoons fresh cilantro

Work fish into small flakes, certain all small bones are removed, set aside. To speed up the preparation time of salsa, use a hand-operated food mixer if available. In a medium bowl, gently mix the remaining ingredients. Add fish and a few leaves of cilantro to the top.

*The light, flaky pastry in these triangles accents the delicate flavors inside. Great served alone or with honey mustard or soy ginger dipping sauce.*

Sauté chopped mushrooms in butter until soft. Work fish into small flakes, certain all bones are removed, set aside. Mix mushrooms, fish, cream cheese, onion and white wine until thoroughly combined. Place one sheet of phyllo on a cutting board. Brush sheet with melted butter, top with a second sheet of phyllo. Cut the double layer of phyllo into 3 equal sections, lengthwise. Place a tablespoon of filling at the bottom of a section.

Diagonally fold phyllo over the filling, taking corner to the opposite edge, like how a flag is rolled up. Continue folding, keeping the triangle shape all the way to end. Place triangle, seam side down, on a baking sheet. Brush the tops of the triangles with melted butter. Bake in a preheated oven at 375° for 12-15 minutes or until triangles are golden brown.

- 1 cup cooked, flaked salmon or steelhead
- 1 cup chopped mushrooms
- 1 tablespoon butter
- 1/3 cup softened cream cheese
- 1/2 teaspoon granulated onion
- 2 tablespoons white wine
- 10 sheets prepared phyllo dough (approximately 9" x 14")
- 1/2 cup melted butter

# Salads & Soups

Salads and soups constitute some of the world's most popular lunch items. At the same time, they are also great for brunch or a light dinner. In addition to a nice flavor, the beauty of preparing fish in this way is the dietary value that is derived. If searching for a way to spice-up a simple dish, or create a full meal, just add some fish to your soups and salads.

# Smokey Penne Pasta Salad

*The ingredients in this salad were meant to go together.
This pasta salad is packed with flavor and is filling
enough to be a meal in itself.*

- 1 cup flaked, smoked salmon or steelhead
- 3 tablespoons pesto sauce (see index for pesto recipe)
- 12-15 spinach leaves
- 1/4 cup roasted red peppers
- 1 cup cubed smoked mozzarella cheese
- 2 cups uncooked penne pasta

Cook pasta as directed on package. Wilt spinach leaves by tossing them in with warm, drained pasta. Cool and set aside. Gently stir pesto sauce into pasta. Work fish into small flakes, certain all small bones are removed. Add fish, peppers and cheese, toss lightly. Serve at room temperature.

# Red Potato Dill Salad

*Devoted potato salad fans will love this twist; the dill brings out the slight salmon flavor in this fresh-tasting salad.*

Boil potatoes in water until tender. Cool completely in refrigerator. Work fish into small flakes, certain all bones are removed, set aside. Cut potatoes into fourths. In a large mixing bowl combine potatoes, celery, onion and fish. In a small bowl, thoroughly mix sour cream, dill, pepper and salt. Gently fold sour cream mixture into potato mixture. Refrigerate until ready to serve.

- 1 cup cooked, flaked salmon or steelhead
- 1 pound red potatoes
- 3 stalks celery, chopped
- 3 stalks green onion, sliced
- 1 cup sour cream
- 2 teaspoons dill
- 1/2 teaspoon salt
- Black pepper to taste

# Macaroni Confetti Salad

*The ingredients in this salad balance well, creating an*
*original tasting, colorful side dish.*

- 1 cup cooked, flaked salmon or steelhead
- 1 4-ounce jar pimentos, drained
- 1 6-ounce can black olives, halved
- 1 cup carrots, sliced
- 1 cup celery, sliced
- 1 1/2 cups mayonnaise
- 1/2 teaspoon celery salt
- 1/2 teaspoon granulated onion
- 1/2 teaspoon garlic powder
- Salt and black pepper to taste
- 2 cups uncooked pasta

Work fish into small flakes, certain all bones are removed, set aside. Cook pasta as directed on package. Cool by running under cold water, drain well. In a large bowl, gently mix pimentos, olives, carrots, celery and fish. In a small bowl, mix mayonnaise, celery salt, onion and garlic. Add to pasta and mix. Salt and pepper to taste.

*Great as a starter, this salad satisfies the hungry while waiting on traditional BBQ fare.*

Chop carrots, zucchini and radish, julienned style. In a medium bowl, mix carrots, zucchini, radish, parsley, capers, olive oil and red wine vinegar. Set aside and let marinate while fish is being prepared. Skin the fillet and slice fish into 1/2" pieces. Pour olive oil onto a saucer. Heat grill to high. Drag fish through olive oil and place on a well-oiled grill. Turn heat to medium. Cook each side 2 minutes or until fish flakes. Try turning only once as this thinly sliced fish is very fragile on the grill. While fish is cooking, place greens on plate. Take fish directly from the grill, top with a portion of the marinated vegetables and serve immediately. Garnish with lime wedges if desired. Makes 4-6 servings.

- 1 8-12-ounce skinned fillet of salmon or steelhead
- 1/3 cup olive oil
- 1/2 cup carrots, julienned
- 1/2 cup zucchini, julienned
- 1/4 cup radish, julienned
- 2 tablespoons fresh parsley
- 3 tablespoons capers
- 1/2 cup olive oil
- 1/4 cup red wine vinegar
- 4-6 cups salad greens
- Lime wedges for garnish

# Crunchy Pea Salad

*A favorite potluck side dish of ours, the addition of fish makes a nice variation that can be made into a light meal on its own.*

- 1 cup cooked, flaked salmon or steelhead
- 1 16-ounce bag of peas
- 3-4 large mushrooms, chopped
- 3 stalks celery, sliced
- 1 5-ounce can water chestnuts, chopped
- 3/4 cup prepared ranch dressing
- 1/2 cup sour cream

Rinse frozen peas in a colander to partially thaw. In a large bowl, mix peas, mushrooms, celery and water chestnuts. In a small bowl, combine ranch dressing and sour cream. Work fish into small flakes, certain all bones are removed, set aside. Add dressing mixture to pea mixture and gently stir in fish. Keep refrigerated until ready to serve.

*Sitting at a sidewalk cafe, people watching and nibbling on Nicoise was a highlight of our stay in Paris. Recreating the salad with salmon or steelhead brings back fond memories.*

Having all of the ingredients in this recipe prepared prior to putting them all together is ideal. All ingredients should be chilled for at least one hour. Steam green beans using either fresh or frozen, French cut, green beans. Boil potatoes until tender. Hard boil eggs and slice onions. Work fish into bite-sized flakes, certain all bones are removed. For the presentation, tear salad greens and divide evenly among serving plates. Evenly distribute remaining ingredients, saving the fish and capers for the final layer.

- 2 cups cooked, flaked salmon or steelhead (can use grilled fish from Grilled Salad recipe)
- 1 cup green beans, French cut
- 1 large can black olives
- 2 medium potatoes, cubed
- 1/2 cup red onions, sliced
- 3-4 hard boiled eggs
- 4-6 tablespoons capers
- 4-6 cups salad greens
- Your favorite vinaigrette salad dressing

# Creamy Salmon Mousse with Marinated Cucumbers

*Cucumbers paired with salmon or steelhead always
make for delightfully fresh summertime fare.*

- 1 1/2 cups smoked salmon
  or steelhead
- 1/2 cup plain yogurt
- 2 tablespoons olive oil
- 2 teaspoons lemon juice
- Salt to taste

MARINATED CUCUMBERS:
- 2 cucumbers
- 1 sweet red mini-pepper
- 1 sweet yellow mini-pepper
- 1/4 cup olive oil
- 2 tablespoons white
  wine vinegar
- 1 teaspoon sugar
- 1/2 teaspoon salt

Work smoked meat into tiny flakes, certain all bones are removed. Add all ingredients to a food processor and mix thoroughly. Serve on a bed of marinated cucumber salad.

MARINATED CUCUMBERS:

In a medium-sized bowl, mix olive oil, white wine vinegar, salt and sugar until sugar is dissolved. Peel and thinly slice cucumbers, placing them directly in the oil and vinegar mix. Thinly slice red and yellow peppers and add to mixture. Cover and refrigerate for 30 minutes to 3 hours.

*Our children call this a "tuna" sandwich without the bread. It is a great use for leftovers from the oven or grill.*

Work fish into small flakes, certain all bones are removed. In a small bowl, add remaining ingredients and stir well. As a time-saver, use a mini-chopper to quickly mix the ingredients. With an ice cream scoop, spoon onto a bed of lettuce.

- **1 cup cooked, flaked salmon or steelhead**
- **2 stalks celery, finely chopped**
- **1 dill pickle, finely chopped**
- **1 teaspoon dried dill**
- **2 teaspoons lemon juice**
- **2/3 cup mayonnaise**

# Waldorf Salad

*An interesting version of an old favorite. Serve on a bed
of fresh salad greens and garnish with a slice of lemon.*

- 1 cup cooked, flaked salmon
  or steelhead
- 1/2 cup celery, chopped
- 1/2 cup apple, peeled
  and diced
- 1 cup red grapes
- 2/3 cup walnuts, coarsely
  chopped
- 1/2 cup mayonnaise
- 1/3 cup sour cream
- 2 teaspoons lemon juice
- 1/2 teaspoon black pepper
- 1/2 teaspoon onion powder
- 1/2 teaspoon salt

Work fish into small flakes, certain all
bones are removed, set aside. In a large
bowl, gently mix celery, apple, grapes,
walnuts and fish. In a small bowl, mix
mayonnaise, sour cream, lemon juice,
pepper, onion powder and salt. Add the
mayonnaise mix to the apple mix and toss.

# Citrus Basil Salad

*Though not the true definition of "tartare", we have found that most people still consider this fish not fully cooked. Served best with very fresh fish, this is a nice, light, tart salad topper.*

Slice fish fillet at a diagonal to get large cuts 1/8" to 1/4" thick. Pour lime juice in a shallow baking dish and distribute fresh basil leaves around the pan. Lay fish slices atop lime and basil mixture. Lightly salt to taste. Cover and refrigerate. Turn fish slices every 15-30 minutes for up to 3 hours. The fish will partially cook in the lime juice due to its acid content but will remain slightly opaque. Serve on a bed of baby lettuce.

- **8-10-ounce skinned salmon or steelhead fillet**
- **3 tablespoons lime or lemon juice**
- **1/4 cup fresh basil leaves**
- **Salt to taste**
- **Baby lettuce**

# Seviche

*A favorite of ours with calamari, we like this version contributed by Chef Ron Schrodt of Eugene, Oregon.*

- 8-10-ounce skinned salmon or steelhead
- 3 tablespoons red onion, minced
- 3 tablespoons chives, minced
- Juice of 1 lemon
- Salt and pepper to taste

Chop salmon into small cubes, making sure all bones are removed. Mix all ingredients. Marinate fish in lemon juice mixture 30 minutes to 2 hours, stirring occasionally. Refrigerate until ready to serve. Serve on a bed of greens with bread or crackers.

*We like coleslaw with bay shrimp, but once used salmon as a substitute and discovered a new salad to enjoy.*

Work fish into small flakes, certain all bones are removed, set aside. In a large mixing bowl, add chopped cabbage, shredded carrot and fish. In a small bowl, mix remaining ingredients for dressing. Gently stir in dressing mix. Refrigerate until ready to serve.

- 1 cup cooked, flaked salmon or steelhead
- 2 cups green cabbage, thinly sliced and chopped
- 1 cup purple cabbage, thinly sliced and chopped
- 1 carrot, shredded
- 1/2 cup sour cream
- 1/4 cup Miracle Whip
- 2 teaspoons sugar
- 2 teaspoons lemon juice
- 1 teaspoon celery salt
- 1 teaspoon dry mustard or substitute home-made dressing for 1 cup ranch dressing

# Potato Leek Soup

*With a fresh bundle of leeks gathered from the garden, this recipe was born. Easy to prepare, this thick, hearty soup is a crowd pleaser.*

- 2 cups cooked, flaked salmon or steelhead
- 1/2 pound bacon, chopped in 1/2" pieces
- 6-8 medium-sized leeks, thinly sliced
- 4 potatoes, peeled and cubed
- 2 stalks celery, chopped
- 2 carrots, sliced
- 4 cups chicken bouillon
- 1 pint heavy cream

In a large soup pot, fry bacon pieces until crisp. Remove bacon and set aside, leaving drippings in pot. Sauté leeks on medium-high heat until soft and translucent. Add cubed potatoes, chopped celery and sliced carrots. Cover and lower heat to medium, cooking until potatoes are tender. Add chicken bouillon and cooked bacon, cover and simmer 15-20 minutes. Remove from heat, add cream and flaked fish. Warm soup to desired temperature taking care not to let boil. Salt and pepper to taste.

# Fish Chowder

*A family favorite, we like putting this in the
Crock Pot before heading to Sunday morning church.
It's a wonderful, wholesome soup to come home to.*

Work fish into small flakes, certain all bones are removed, set aside. Cut bacon into 1" squares. In a large skillet, fry bacon until crisp. Remove bacon from grease and set aside. Add chopped onions to bacon grease and cook over medium heat until onions are translucent. Add garlic and diced potatoes. Sprinkle flour into pan, constantly stirring. Cook until potatoes are soft. If needed, add a few tablespoons of butter to keep potatoes from sticking. Mix into skillet the diced ham, fish and cooked bacon (save a bit of bacon for garnish if desired). Add milk and cook 5-10 minutes, continually stirring. Salt and pepper to taste. If desired, chowder can be placed in Crock Pot on low heat and left safely for several hours. Or cover the chowder and continue heating on medium-low heat 25-30 minutes or until desired thickness is attained. Stir in parsley just before serving. Garnish with cooked bacon.

- 2 cups cooked, flaked salmon or steelhead
- 1 pound bacon
- 1 cup diced ham
- 1 onion, diced
- 2 cloves garlic, minced
- 1/4 cup flour
- 6 cups potatoes, peeled and diced
- 6 cups milk
- Butter, if needed
- Salt and pepper to taste
- 2 tablespoons fresh parsley, coarsely chopped
- Bacon bits for garnish

# Cream of Celery Soup

*With the varieties fish you can choose to add, this soup
is very versatile. Fresh herbs are also a nice addition.*

- 1/2 cup herbed gravlax or smoked salmon
- 2 tablespoons butter
- 1 1/2 cups chopped celery
- 1/2 cup chopped onion
- 2 cups chicken broth
- 1 cup milk
- 1/2 cup sour cream
- 1/2 teaspoon salt

Melt butter in a large stock pot. Add celery and onions and sauté until onions are translucent. Add chicken broth, bring to a boil. Simmer on low heat 15-20 minutes. Add milk, sour cream and salt. Bring to desired temperature. Garnish with thinly sliced herbed gravlax or small chunks of smoked salmon.

# Salmon Bisque

*This lightly flavored soup is a nice starter
for any seafood-based menu.*

Place fish, broth, onion, celery, tomatoes, bay leaves, Adobo and peppercorns in a medium sauce pan. Bring to boiling and turn heat down to low. Simmer, uncovered for 30-45 minutes. Run soup through a strainer and set aside. Discard all but the broth. Melt butter in a medium sauce pan on medium-high heat. Slowly whisk flour in with the butter. Once the butter and flour mixture are bubbly, slowly add milk using the whisk to thoroughly mix. When the milk mixture starts to boil, add strained broth mixture. Heat throughout, season with salt and pepper and serve immediately. Garnish with smoked salmon.

- 2 salmon or steelhead steaks or an 8-ounce fillet
- 2 cups chicken broth
- 1 cup water
- 1 medium onion, chopped
- 3 stalks celery, chopped
- 2 tomatoes, chopped
- 2 bay leaves
- 10 peppercorns
- 1 teaspoon Adobo
- 1/4 cup butter
- 1/4 cup flour
- 2 cups whole milk
- Salt and pepper to taste
- Smoked salmon for garnish

# Entrees

When it comes to entrees, most people who routinely cook salmon and steelhead seem to have a favorite signature dish. Because entrees are a joy to create, and better yet, savor the taste of, this section draws upon the expertise of many devoted cooks; ones who were willing to share their esteemed recipe. Following is a collection of entrees sure to appeal to anyone who loves fish, or who has always been somewhat skeptical in overcoming that "fish" taste.

# Green Pepper Bacon Crusted

*The sour cream topping makes for a rich, appetizing
fish entree that nicely accompanies baked potatoes.*

- 1 fillet of salmon or steelhead
  (3-6 servings)
- 1/2 pound thick-sliced bacon,
  cut into 1/2" pieces
- 1/2 cup onion, chopped
- 3/4 cup sour cream
- 1/2 cup green pepper, diced
- Salt and pepper to taste

Fry bacon until crisp, drain on a paper
towel. Leave bacon grease in frying pan and
sauté onions until translucent. Remove
onions with a slotted spoon and set aside.
Mix onions, sour cream, green pepper and
1/2 the bacon in a small bowl and cover the
fish fillet. (Any remaining sour cream
mixture can be used to garnish the
potatoes.) Bake in preheated oven at 350°
for 25 minutes or until fish is opaque and
flakes in large chunks. Garnish fillet with
remaining cooked bacon.

# Poached Salmon With Beurre Noir

*An easy entree to prepare, the sauce adds a nice, sophisticated taste to the fish. To date this is one of Scott's favorite ways to eat salmon and steelhead.*

Place fish in a large frying pan or skillet. Add onion, parsley and black pepper and cover with water. Heat to a gentle boil. Reduce heat to medium and simmer 20 minutes or until fish is opaque and flakes in large chunks. Remove fish from saucepan and place on a serving plate. Set aside and make sauce. Melt butter in a sauce pan on high heat. When butter begins to brown, remove from heat and add capers, vinegar and parsley. Pour sauce over fish and serve immediately.

- 1 skinned fillet of salmon or steelhead (3-6 servings)
- 1 small onion cut into fourths
- 4 stalks parsley
- 1/4 teaspoon freshly ground black pepper

BEURRE NOIR:
- 4 tablespoons butter
- 2 tablespoons vinegar
- 2 tablespoons capers
- 1 tablespoon fresh chopped parsley

# Steelhead en Papillote

*French for "baked in parchment paper," this simple method makes for a very moist fish and easy kitchen clean up. As long as the oven stays under 350°, parchment can be substituted for aluminum foil when baking any fish.*

- 1 fillet salmon or steelhead (3-6 servings)
- 2 cloves garlic, minced
- 3-4 slices fresh ginger
- 2 tablespoons melted butter
- Salt to taste
- Fresh chives for garnish

Lay fillet, skin side down, on a large sheet of parchment paper. Salt fillet to taste. Distribute garlic and ginger over the fillet. Drizzle melted butter over the fillet. Fold over edges of paper several times to seal the fish. Place on a baking sheet. Bake at 350° for 15-20 minutes or until fish is opaque and flakes in large chunks.

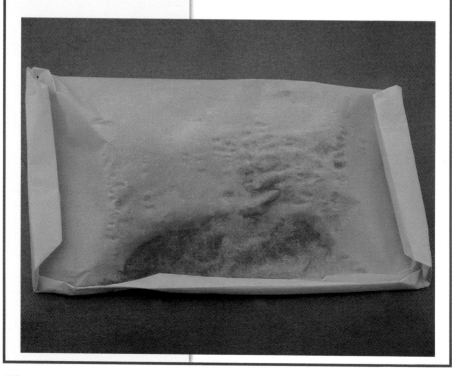

*Nicely crusted with flavorful parmesan, this baked fish is moist and flavorful.*

Place fish fillet on aluminum foil or parchment paper. Spread with parmesan garlic butter. Refrigerate until butter mixture is firm. Place sliced tomatoes on top of the butter mixture. Fold over edges of paper or foil several times to seal the fish. Place on a baking sheet. Bake in a preheated oven at 400° 10 minutes per inch of thickness, or until fish is opaque and flakes in large chunks.

PARMESAN GARLIC BUTTER:
Thoroughly mix all ingredients.

- 1 skinned fillet of salmon or steelhead (3-6 servings)
- Sliced tomatoes

PARMESAN GARLIC BUTTER:
- 1/2 cup butter, softened to room temperature
- 3 cloves garlic, minced
- 1/2 cup parmesan cheese
- 1 teaspoon Italian seasoning

# Feta Cheese Bake

*Strong and flavorful, feta cheese highlights this dish imparting a unique flavor unlike many traditional preparations.*

- 1 fillet of salmon or steelhead (3-6 servings)
- 2 tablespoons mayonnaise
- 1 tablespoon sour cream
- 1 tablespoon white wine vinegar
- 1 tablespoon milk
- 2 tablespoons feta cheese
- 1/4 teaspoon granulated onion
- 1/4 teaspoon garlic powder
- 1/4 teaspoon dill
- 1/4 teaspoon celery salt
- 1/8 teaspoon white pepper
- 1/2 teaspoon freshly ground anise seeds
- 2-3 tablespoons feta cheese (for the top)

Lay fish fillet, skin side down, on a foil-wrapped baking dish. In a small bowl, mix all of the above ingredients, except for the feta cheese. Bake fish in a preheated oven at 400° for 10 minutes. Remove fish from oven and spread the mayonnaise mixture over the fish. Top with remaining feta cheese. Bake an additional 5-10 minutes or until feta cheese topping is golden brown and fish is opaque and flakes in large chunks. Top with more freshly ground anise if desired.

# Sesame Dill Salmon

*Simple and fast, this recipe has a nice flavor and texture.*

Place salmon fillet in a greased broiling pan or a metal baking dish (do not use a glass pan as the broiler may get too hot). In a small frying pan, melt butter on medium heat. Add sesame seeds and sauté until golden brown. Add dill, stir, and remove from heat. Coat fish with the sesame dill mixture. Broil 9-10 minutes, watching closely.

- 1 skinned fillet of salmon or steelhead (3-6 servings)
- 1/4 cup of butter
- 3 tablespoons sesame seeds
- 1 tablespoon dill weed

# Lightly Lemon Poached

*One of the healthiest ways to cook salmon, the light flavor works for fish served hot or cold.*

- 1 skinned fillet of salmon or steelhead (3-6 servings)
- Juice of 2 fresh squeezed lemons
- 1/2 teaspoon salt

Place fish in a frying pan or skillet. Cover with water, lemon juice and salt. Heat to a gentle boil. Reduce heat to medium and simmer 20 minutes or until fish is opaque and flakes in large chunks. Remove fish from pan and place on a serving plate. Grind black pepper over fillet if desired. If fish is to be served cold, cover and refrigerate at least 2 hours and up to 24 hours.

# Bacon-Wrapped Salmon

*Although this recipe takes the low-fat out of salmon and steelhead, cooking it adds the appealing flavor of bacon and makes an easy main entree.*

Place fish fillet skin side down. Sprinkle with onion salt. Lay strips of bacon over fish, covering fully. Bake in a 400° preheated oven for 10 minutes per inch of fillet thickness or until fish is opaque and flakes in large chunks. Turn oven to broil for an additional 1-2 minutes (watch closely) to crisp the bacon. Serve immediately.

- 1 fillet of salmon or steelhead (3-6 servings)
- 1/2 pound sliced bacon
- Onion salt

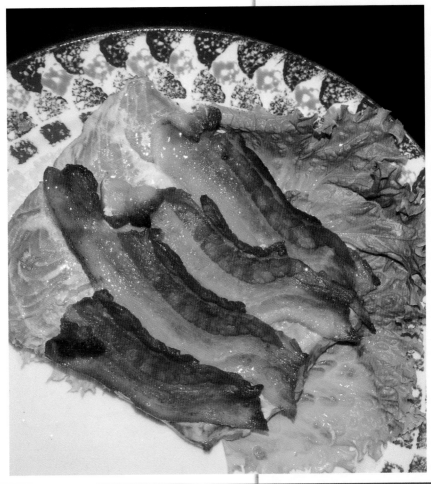

# Indoor Grilled With Tropical Salsa

*One of the most useful Christmas presents we have received is our George Foreman Lean Mean Grilling Machine. With all the great tastes we put on fish, our oldest son, Braxton, still prefers a lightly seasoned fillet grilled indoors.*

- 1 skinned fillet of salmon or steelhead (3-6 servings)
- Salt and pepper to taste
- Cooking spray

TROPICAL SALSA:

- 1 cup papaya, peeled and chopped
- 1 cup mango, pitted, peeled and chopped
- 1 avocado, pitted, peeled and chopped
- 1 red bell pepper, diced
- 2 teaspoons fresh mint
- 2 tablespoons orange juice
- 2 tablespoons lime juice
- 2 teaspoons canola oil

Preheat grill at "minimum" temperature setting. Spray top and bottom of grill with nonstick cooking spray. Place fillets on grill, lightly season and close lid. Cook fillets 4-6 minutes depending on thickness. Salmon or steelhead steaks can also be prepared on this grill with an increased cooking time of 10-12 minutes.

TROPICAL SALSA:

In a large bowl combine all ingredients. Cover and refrigerate at least 30 minutes.

# 1,000 Island Fish

*This tasty, timesaving recipe comes from good friend
Sandi Jacobson and is one of the quickest in the book
to prepare. It's great for baking or grilling.*

Place fish, skin side down, on aluminum foil. Cover fillet in lemon juice. Spread a thick layer of salad dressing over fish. Bake in a preheated oven at 350° 15-25 minutes or until fish is opaque and flakes in large chunks.

- 1 fillet of salmon or steelhead (3-6 servings)
- 1/2 cup prepared Thousand Island salad dressing
- 2 tablespoons lemon juice concentrate, or the juice of 1 lemon

# Sweet & Spicy Fish

*The sweet and slightly hot, exotic flavors in this rub offer
a nice change of pace from everyday baked fish.*

- 1 skinned fillet of salmon or steelhead (3-6 servings)
- 1/3 cup water
- 1/3 cup orange juice concentrate
- 3 tablespoons lemon juice concentrate, or the juice from 1 lemon
- 1 tablespoon brown sugar
- 2 teaspoons chili powder
- Rind from 1 lemon
- 1/2 teaspoon cumin
- 1/2 teaspoon salt
- 1/4 teaspoon cinnamon

Combine water, orange juice concentrate and lemon juice in a shallow pan and marinate for 1-3 hours, occasionally turning fish. Mix remaining ingredients to use as the rub. Remove fish from marinade and coat each side in the rub mixture. Bake in a preheated oven at 400° 10 minutes per inch of thickness or until fish is opaque and flakes in large chunks.

# Wild Blackberry Glazed

*This signature dish comes from Don Homuth, avid Oregon angler and devoted Northwest Steelheader Association member.*

Run blackberries through a sieve to remove seeds. In a large stock pot, cook berries down to equal approximately 4 cups of puree. Add sugar and cook over medium heat until sugar is dissolved. Unless you plan to use the blackberry syrup within a week, you will need to can it. Put blackberry syrup in clean canning jars, adjust lids and give them a 10-15-minute bath in boiling water. Each batch may set up differently; if syrupy, brush on, if thick, add water then brush on.

Put fish, skin side down, on aluminum foil and brush lightly with cooking oil. Glaze with blackberry syrup 3-5 times during the baking or grilling process. Bake in a preheated oven at 400° 10 minutes per inch of thickness or until fish is opaque and flakes in large chunks.

- **1 skinned fillet of salmon or steelhead (3-6 servings)**
- **2 gallons blackberries**
- **7 cups sugar**
- **Cooking oil**

# Strawberry BBQ Glazed

*Growing up on a strawberry farm, Tiffany had about every possible strawberry dish imaginable. This recipe makes a beautiful presentation, offering a sweet, tangy flavor.*

- 4-6 salmon or steelhead steaks
- 1/2 cup sliced strawberries (may use fresh or frozen)
- 1/4 cup of your favorite BBQ sauce
- 1 tablespoon canola oil
- 1 tablespoon water
- 1/4 teaspoon salt
- 1/4 teaspoon white pepper
- 1/4 cup butter
- 1 Walla Walla onion, thinly sliced
- 3-4 sprigs fresh cilantro

In a blender or food processor, blend strawberries, oil, water, salt and pepper until smooth. Melt butter in a medium sauce pan, add onions and sauté until translucent. The longer the onions are sautéed, the sweeter they will become. It is nice to have a very sweet onion to accompany the strawberry glaze. Place steaks on a well-greased broiler pan. Brush steaks with strawberry glaze. Broil for 2 minutes under a preheated broiler 4" from the heat. Glaze again, broil 2 more minutes and turn steaks over. Repeat the glazing on the other side. Garnish with fresh cilantro and strawberries if desired.

# Blackened Fish

*While Justin and Nikki Aamodt, of Diamond A Guides in Burns, Oregon, specialize in big- and small-game hunting, they are both tremendous cooks of fish and game. This is their favorite way to eat salmon and steelhead, and one worth trying.*

Mix all dry ingredients in a small bowl. In a pie pan or shallow dish sprinkle dry mixture over the bottom. Heat a cast-iron skillet or regular frying pan on medium-high heat. Make sure the pan is completely dry. When the pan is hot, dip fish fillets into mixture covering both sides. Cook approximately 4 minutes per side and serve.

- 4 8-ounce fillets of skinned salmon or steelhead
- 2 teaspoons unsweetened cocoa powder
- 1 teaspoon cinnamon
- 2 teaspoons granulated onion or onion powder
- 2 teaspoons salt
- 1 teaspoon black pepper
- 4 teaspoons white sugar
- 1-2 crushed juniper berries (optional)

# Salmon Patties With Ginger Soy Sauce

*Large patties can be served alone or on a bun, and smaller patties can be made for a wonderful appetizer.*

- 1 cup cooked, flaked salmon or steelhead
- 2/3 cup dried bread crumbs
- 1 egg, beaten
- 1/3 cup milk
- 1 green onion, finely chopped
- 1 tablespoon dill weed
- 1/4 teaspoon salt
- 1/4 teaspoon black pepper
- 2 tablespoons vegetable oil

### Soy Ginger Sauce:

- 1/3 cup mayonnaise
- 1 tablespoon fresh ginger
- 1/2 tablespoon soy sauce
- 1 clove garlic
- 1 tablespoon rice vinegar

Work fish into small flakes, certain all bones are removed, set aside. Combine fish, bread crumbs, egg, milk, chopped onion, dill weed, salt and pepper in a bowl and mix thoroughly. Heat oil in a large skillet over medium heat. Shape mixture into 4 large patties or 8 to 10 small patties. Cook patties about 4 minutes on each side, turning only once, until golden brown.

### Soy Ginger Sauce:

Puree in a blender or food processor until smooth. Spread on hamburger buns or use as a sauce for the patties.

# Beer-Battered Salmon Sticks

*This rather nontraditional way of serving salmon and steelhead is popular among those who like deep-fried foods. Finger foods such as this are favorites with our kids and their friends.*

Mix flour and salt in a wide-brimmed bowl. Add oil, egg and beer, then mix. Batter may be slightly lumpy, do not over mix. Rinse and pat strips of fish dry. Heat shortening in a deep frying pan on medium-high heat, or an electric fry pan at 350°. Once shortening has liquified and heated, dip fish strips one at a time into batter mixture. Carefully laying fish into pan, take care not to put strips too close together. Cook 4-5 minutes, until golden brown, on each side. Drain on a wire rack or paper towels. Serve hot with dip (mix of 3 parts mayonnaise to 1 part ketchup).

- 1 salmon or steelhead fillet, skinned and cut into 1 1/2" strips
- 1 cup flour
- 1 teaspoon salt
- 1 tablespoon oil
- 1 egg
- 3/4 cup regular or nonalcoholic beer
- 1 cup shortening for frying

# Braxton's Fettuccine

*Move over macaroni and cheese, our sons refer to this recipe as, "Slurpy noodles with cheese." Sometimes we even sneak in some "green chunks" from the garden, such as zucchini, broccoli or baby spinach leaves.*

- 1/2 pound cooked flaked salmon or steelhead (left over from the BBQ works great)
- 1/2 cup butter
- 1 clove garlic
- 3/4 cup heavy cream
- 1/2 cup milk
- 1/2 cup Mozzarella cheese
- 1/4 cup parmesan cheese
- 1/4 cup Monterey Jack cheese
- 1/2 teaspoon pepper
- 1/2 teaspoon salt
- 12 ounces cooked fettuccine

Melt butter in a saucepan, add garlic and sauté. Blend in cream, milk, cheeses, salt and pepper. Heat on medium, stirring constantly, until thickened. Add salmon and heat thoroughly. Pour over fettuccine, toss lightly and serve.

# Smokey Linguine

*Bob Cobb of Bob Cobb's Reel Fishing Trips in Reedsport, Oregon is one of the state's most accomplished anglers. His wife, Peggy, prepares several fish meals a week for the family. This is one of Peggy's finest recipes, and one of our all-time favorite pasta dishes.*

Work fish into small flakes, certain all bones are removed, set aside. Melt butter in a heavy skillet, add cream and reduce, stirring constantly until thickened. Add smoked salmon, parmesan cheese, pepper and parsley. Simmer 10 minutes, meanwhile, cooking linguine to desired tenderness. Toss together and serve.

- 1 cup smoked salmon or steelhead
- 8 tablespoons butter
- 1 cup whipping cream
- 3/4 cup parmesan cheese
- 2 tablespoons parsley
- Pepper to taste
- 8 ounces linguine

# Herb Roasted Salmon With Tarragon Sauce

*We first learned of this fascinating recipe from* Fish Alaska *Magazine, one of the country's fastest growing sport fishing periodicals. It was given to them by Kenai River Raven Lodge located in Soldotna, Alaska, the king salmon capitol of the world.*

- 1 skinned fillet of salmon
- 1 fresh lemon sliced
- 1/4 cup pure virgin olive oil
- 2 teaspoons fresh chopped garlic
- 9 sprigs fresh lemon basil
- 3 sprigs fresh tarragon leaves
- 4 sprigs fresh mint
- 3 sprigs fresh lemon mint
- 6 fresh chervil leaves
- 1 sprig fresh rosemary

**Note:** You may substitute commercially available "fish medley" herb package for other herbs, except fresh tarragon, for the sauce.

- 1/2 cup half-and-half
- 1/2 cup heavy whipping cream
- 1 sprig fresh tarragon
- Kosher salt and fresh ground pepper to taste

Preheat oven to 375°. Cover a flat 1 1/2" to 2" deep ovenproof pan with aluminum foil. Build a shell out of more foil and set fish inside. Squeeze 2 slices of fresh lemon on fish and drizzle with pure virgin olive oil. Sprinkle with kosher salt and fresh ground pepper. Place remaining lemon slices on fish. Cover with blanket of fresh herb combination and enclose fillet within the foil shell. Bake for 15 to 18 minutes. When fish is done, remove herbs from top, reserving juice. Pour juice into a sauce pan and add half-and-half and heavy whipping cream, stir until thickened. Add chopped tarragon, kosher salt and fresh ground pepper to taste. Just before serving, pour a little sauce over fish and serve hot.

# Grilled Salmon in Pistachio Herb Butter

*This special recipe also comes from* Fish Alaska Magazine, *as given to them by Simon & Seaforts Saloon & Grill in Anchorage, Alaska.*

Butter and season both sides of fish, place on broiler at medium heat. Grill until 125°. Baste liberally with butter and season again lightly as you serve the fish. Squeeze lemon wedge over fish. Garnish with thinly sliced lemons and sprigs of fresh rosemary and thyme.

PISTACHIO HERB BUTTER:

Whip butter until light, add balance of ingredients and mix well. Refrigerate until needed.

- 1 skinned fillet of salmon
- 4 ounces pistachio herb butter (recipe follows)
- 2 teaspoons salt
- 1 teaspoon fresh ground black pepper
- 1 lemon, cut into 6 wedges (4 to squeeze on the fish, 2 thin slices for garnish)

PISTACHIO HERB BUTTER:
- 1 pound butter, softened
- 1/4 pound chopped, toasted pistachios
- 1/2 ounce fresh, minced garlic
- 1/8 ounce fresh, minced rosemary
- 1/16 ounce roughly chopped fresh thyme
- 1/2 ounce roughly chopped fresh basil
- 1 tablespoon Worcestershire sauce
- 1 1/2 teaspoon dry mustard
- 1/2 ounce minced fresh shallots
- 2 drops liquid smoke
- 1 tablespoon minced fresh parsley

# Salmon With Horseradish Crust & Cucumber Relish

*Another* Fish Alaska *Magazine recipe people love. This one came from The Glacier Brewhouse in Anchorage, Alaska. If devoting time to a fancy dish or a dinner party, this is worth a try.*

- 1 1/2 pounds fresh salmon cut into four, 6-ounce fillets
- 1 cup seasoned flour
- 2 beaten eggs
- Salt and pepper

HORSERADISH BUTTER:
- 1/2 pound softened butter
- 2 tablespoons minced shallots
- 2 tablespoons chopped Italian parsley
- 2 teaspoons minced garlic
- 1/4 cup Beaver brand horseradish
- 1 tablespoon fresh lemon juice
- 2 tablespoons stone-ground mustard
- Salt to taste

HORSERADISH CRUST:
- 4 cups fresh bread crumbs
- 1/2 cup fresh herb mix (basil, parsley)
- 1 cup fresh grated horseradish
- 1/2 cup olive oil
- 1 tablespoon seasoned salt

CUCUMBER CHAMPAGNE RELISH:
- 2 cups Brut Champagne
- 2 ounces white vinegar
- 1 1/2 ounces sugar

THIS RECIPE IS DIVIDED INTO SEVERAL PARTS.

HORSERADISH BUTTER:
Whip butter until light and fluffy. Add all other ingredients, cover and hold until ready for use.

HORSERADISH CRUST:
Place all dry ingredients in a bowl and toss together. Add fresh horseradish and toss, slowly drizzle in olive oil. Cover and refrigerate until ready to use.

CUCUMBER CHAMPAGNE RELISH:
Bring vinegar, salt, water, champagne, and sugar to a boil, and stir until sugar and salt are dissolved. Place 2 of the 4 tablespoons of chopped mint in a glass or small stainless-steel bowl, and pour the hot liquid over them. Allow to marinate at least 2 hours. Strain the liquid, discard the mint. Chill. Add to the chilled liquid, the remaining mint, red bell pepper, julienned cucumber and gently stir. Refrigerate.

MINT SOUR CREAM:
Mix all ingredients together in a small bowl. Cover and refrigerate until ready to use.

### FINAL PREPARATION AND ASSEMBLY

Season the salmon with salt and pepper, dredge in the seasoned flour mix, then dip in the egg mix. Place pieces on a baking sheet and cover with the soft horseradish butter. Coat salmon with the bread crumb mix. Bake in a preheated 350° oven for twenty minutes or until the internal temperature of the fish is 120°. Do not overcook. Serve over steamed jasmine rice. Place the relish at the top of the salmon. Top with the mint sour cream. Garnish with 3 chive spears fanned out.

- Dash of salt
- 4 tablespoons fresh chopped mint leaves and stems
- 1 English cucumber, halved and julienne sliced 1/2" thick
- 1 red bell pepper, julienne sliced

### MINT SOUR CREAM:
- 1 cup sour cream
- 1 cup Best Foods Mayonnaise
- 4 tablespoons fresh chopped mint zest and juice from 1 lemon

## *Blackened Salmon With Hollandaise Shrimp Creole Sauce*

*Another unique recipe provided by* Fish Alaska *Magazine, the creator of this one comes from the famous Millennium Alaskan Hotel in the beautiful city of Anchorage, Alaska. This is another gourmet recipe that's fun to try and well worth the effort.*

- **1/2 pound (2 sticks) unsalted butter, melted in a skillet**
- **6 (8-10 ounce) salmon or steelhead fillets**

SEASONING MIX:

- **1 tablespoon sweet paprika**
- **2 1/2 teaspoons salt**
- **1 teaspoon onion powder**
- **1 teaspoon garlic powder**
- **1 teaspoon cayenne pepper**
- **3/4 teaspoon white pepper**
- **3/4 teaspoon black pepper**
- **1/2 teaspoon dry thyme leaves**
- **1/2 teaspoon dry oregano leaves**

Heat a large cast-iron skillet over very high heat until it's beyond the smoking stage and you see white ash in the skillet bottom, at least 10 minutes (the skillet cannot be too hot for this dish). Meanwhile, pour 2 tablespoons melted butter into 6 small ramekins. Set aside and keep warm. Reserve the remaining butter in its skillet. Heat the serving plates in a 250° oven. Thoroughly combine the seasoning mix ingredients in a small bowl. Dip each fillet in the melted butter so that both sides are well coated; then sprinkle seasoning, mix generously and evenly on both sides, patting it in by hand. Place in the hot skillet and pour 1/4 tablespoon melted butter on top of each fillet (be careful, as the butter may flame up). Cook, uncovered, over the same high heat until the underside looks charred, about 1 to 1 1/2 minutes (the time will vary according to the fillet thickness and the heat of the skillet). Turn the fillets over and again, pour butter on top, cook until done. Repeat with the remaining fillets. Serve each fillet on top of the Hollandaise sauce with a ramekin of butter on a heated serving plate.

HOLLANDAISE SHRIMP CREOLE SAUCE:

Melt slowly and keep 1/2 cup butter warm. Barely heat 1 1/2 tablespoons lemon juice, dry sherry or tarragon vinegar. Have ready a small saucepan of boiling water and a tablespoon with which to measure it when ready. Place egg yolks in the top of a double boiler, over not in, hot water. Beat 3 egg yolks with a wire whisk until they begin to thicken. Add 1 tablespoon of the boiling water. Beat again until the eggs begin to thicken. Repeat this process until you have added 3 more tablespoons of water. Beat in the warm lemon juice, sherry or vinegar. Remove double boiler from heat. Beat the sauce well with a wire whisk. Continue to beat while slowly adding butter, 1/4 teaspoon salt, 1/4 cup diced green onion, 1/4 cup bay shrimp, 1/4 cup diced ham, 2 tablespoons Cajun spice mix, 1/4 cup diced tomatoes. This sauce also goes great with any kind of seafood or beef.

# One-Dish Meals

*T*he beauty of one-dish meals is the ease with which
they can be created. They lend themselves nicely to
working with leftovers or canned fish. Because
these meals keep well, they can be made ahead
of time and require little planning.
They serve many people, or can be put
aside as leftovers themselves.

# Colorful Orzo Medley

*Vibrant and fresh tasting, this dish will be the center of attention at any meal. It travels well for a great take-along side dish.*

- 1 1/2 cups cooked, flaked salmon or steelhead
- 2 tablespoons olive oil
- 2 tablespoons butter
- 1/4 cup sweet onions, finely diced
- 2 cloves garlic, minced
- 1 cup uncooked orzo pasta
- 1 can chicken broth
- 2/3 cup carrots, sliced and lightly steamed
- 1 red bell pepper, diced
- 1 cup green beans, fresh or frozen
- 1 14.5-ounce can Italian stewed tomatoes, with liquid
- 1/2 teaspoon turmeric
- 1/2 teaspoon salt
- 1/4 teaspoon white pepper
- 1 tablespoon fresh basil
- 2 tablespoons fresh parsley
- 1/4 cup grated parmesan cheese

Separate fish into bite-sized pieces, certain all small bones are removed, set aside. Steam sliced carrots 2-4 minutes in a microwave. Melt butter in a large skillet over medium heat. Add olive oil. Add onions, garlic and orzo to the butter and olive oil. Turn heat to medium-high and brown the orzo, stirring constantly, about 3-5 minutes. Add vegetables, sautéing lightly, about 5 minutes. Gently stir in turmeric, salt, pepper, tomatoes and chicken broth. Cover and reduce heat. Simmer 10 minutes. Add fish and continue cooking until liquid is absorbed. Remove from heat, toss in basil and parsley and top with parmesan cheese.

# Mushroom & Rice Bake

*Comfort food at its finest, this dish is one of those that tastes even better the next day.*

Separate fish into bite-sized pieces, certain all bones are removed, set aside. Melt butter in a medium skillet. Add peppers and sauté 2-4 minutes. Add mushrooms and squash and sauté an additional 2-3 minutes. In a large mixing bowl, whisk together the soup and the milk. Add all remaining ingredients and 1/2 cup of the French-fried onions, stir just to combine. Take special care not to break up the fish. Pour into a buttered, 9" by 11" casserole pan. Bake, uncovered, in a preheated oven at 350° for 30-35 minutes or until heated throughout. Sprinkle the remaining French- fried onions on the casserole during the last 10 minutes of cooking time.

- 1 1/2 cups cooked or smoked, flaked salmon or steelhead
- 4 tablespoons butter
- 1 green pepper, diced
- 1 pound mushrooms, diced
- 1 zucchini squash, diced
- 1 can cream of mushroom soup
- 1/2 cup milk
- 3 cups cooked rice
- 1 cup French-fried onions, divided
- Black pepper to taste

# Thick-Crust Pizza

*This dish brings out the versatility of salmon and steelhead.*
*It is great with any prepared fish or leftovers.*

- 1 14" round prepared pizza crust (recipe follows)

SAUCE:

- 1 cup cottage cheese
- 2 tablespoons sour cream
- 1 egg
- 1 teaspoon oregano
- 3 cloves garlic

TOPPINGS:

- 3-4 ounces gravlax or smoked or cooked, flaked salmon or steelhead
- 1/2 cup sliced zucchini
- 1/2 cup wilted spinach leaves
- 1/3 cup sliced red onion
- 2 tablespoons mozzarella cheese
- 1 tablespoon parmesan cheese
- Corn meal

HERBED PIZZA CRUST:

- 2/3 cup water
- 1 tablespoon olive oil
- 1 3/4 cup bread-machine flour
- 1 teaspoon sugar
- 2 tablespoons parmesan cheese
- 1 teaspoon onion flakes
- 1 teaspoon Italian seasoning
- 1 teaspoon active dry yeast

Prepare pizza crust. Sprinkle pizza stone or pizza pan with corn meal, placing dough on top and set aside. In a food processor, mix sauce ingredients until smooth. Spread evenly on pizza dough, leaving about a 1/2" along the edges. Place toppings evenly on pizza in one layer. Sprinkle with mozzarella and parmesan cheese. Bake in a preheated oven at 425° for 18-22 minutes or until top of pizza is golden brown and crust is browned on the bottom. Time will vary with oven and pan type.

HERBED PIZZA CRUST:

Place ingredients in bread machine in the order they are listed. Follow bread-machine instructions with the dial set to "dough."

# *Easy Oven Omelet*

*We like starting our day with a healthy breakfast.
The eggs and fish in this dish offer a great protein
boost and the veggies are packed with vitamins.*

Heat oven to 325°. Place butter in a glass pie pan and put in the oven. Beat eggs, milk and yogurt until frothy. Remove hot pie pan from the oven. Pour egg mixture into pan and evenly sprinkle gravlax, peppers and onions over the top. Bake at 325° for 15 minutes or until eggs are set. Remove from the oven and sprinkle cheese over the top. Serve in pie-shaped wedges.

- 3 tablespoons herbed gravlax, diced (see index for gravlax recipe)
- 2 tablespoons butter
- 5 eggs
- 1/4 cup milk
- 2 tablespoons plain yogurt
- 3 mini sweet peppers, finely diced
- 1 tablespoon green onion, sliced
- 2 tablespoons grated colby-jack cheese

# Kazden Scramble

*Fresh fish tastes great with a few veggies in scrambled eggs.*
*This is our youngest son's favorite breakfast.*

- 6-10 ounces fresh salmon or steelhead, skinned and deboned
- 6 eggs
- 1/3 cup milk
- 15-20 spinach leaves
- 1/4 cup chopped sweet peppers
- 1 tablespoon olive oil
- Salt and pepper to taste

Chop fish into bite-sized chunks. In a medium skillet, heat the oil on medium-high heat. Sauté fish 3-4 minutes or until opaque, toss in spinach leaves and peppers, sautéing an additional minute. Remove everything from pan and set aside. With a wire whisk, whip eggs and milk until frothy, add salt and pepper to taste. Cook scrambled eggs in the medium skillet, adding the fish and vegetables during the last minute of cooking time. Garnish with mini-sweet pepper rings if desired.

# Couscous-Stuffed Peppers

*Aromatic and healthy, this dish offers an
alternative to the traditional preparation.*

Wash peppers and remove stems. Cut the tops off the peppers and discard all seeds. Separate fish into bite-sized pieces, certain all small bones are removed, set aside. Make couscous as instructed on package. Add vegetables and spices to cooked couscous, mix well.

Arrange peppers in a 9" x 13" baking pan. Fill with stuffing taking care not to pack the mixture down. Pour 1 cup hot water into the bottom of the baking pan. Drizzle 2 tablespoons olive oil over the peppers. Cover tightly with foil. Bake in a preheated oven at 350° for 45-50 minutes or until peppers are tender. Serve with a wedge of lime.

- 1 cup cooked, flaked
  salmon or steelhead
- 6 red, yellow or green
  bell peppers
- 3 cups cooked couscous
- 1/4 cup carrot, grated
- 1/4 cup peas
- 1/2 cup zucchini, chopped
- Pepper tops, chopped
- 2 tablespoons pine nuts
- 1 teaspoon salt
- 1/2 teaspoon coriander
- 1/2 teaspoon turmeric
- 1/4 teaspoon ginger
- 1/4 teaspoon cumin
- 1/8 teaspoon white pepper
- 1/8 teaspoon ground cloves
- 2 tablespoons olive oil
- Lime wedges for garnish

# Spinach Lasagna

*Of the dozen or so types of lasagna Tiffany enjoys preparing, this one is a family favorite. In this dish, the fish is more a source of added protein, not one of dominating flavor.*

- 2 cups cooked, flaked salmon or steelhead
- 1/2 cup butter
- 3 cloves chopped garlic
- 1/2 cup flour
- 2 cups milk
- 1 14-ounce can chicken broth
- 2 cups cottage cheese
- 1 egg
- 2 tablespoons fresh chopped parsley
- 1/2 teaspoon lemon pepper
- 1 bunch spinach, washed and dried
- 9 uncooked lasagna noodles
- 2 cups shredded mozzarella cheese
- 1/2 cup parmesan cheese
- Fresh chives for garnish

Separate fish into bite-sized pieces, certain all bones are removed, set aside. Melt butter in a medium-sized saucepan on medium-low heat. Lightly sauté garlic and add flour, stirring constantly with a wire whisk. When mixture begins to bubble, turn heat to low and slowly add the milk and chicken broth. Return the mixture to a boil until thick, 1-2 minutes, stirring constantly. Remove from heat and set aside.

In a separate bowl, mix the cottage cheese, egg, parsley and lemon pepper. In a 9" x 13" casserole dish, spread enough of the white sauce to coat the bottom of the pan. Layer with 3 uncooked lasagna noodles, 1/3 of the cottage cheese mixture, 1/3 of the spinach, 1/3 of the fish, 1/3 of the mozzarella and parmesan cheeses. Repeat the layering 2 more times, making sure cheese is the final layer.

Bake, uncovered, in a preheated oven at 350° for 50-60 minutes. Let stand at least 10 minutes before serving. Garnish with fresh chives.

# Salmon Tart

*Like a quiche, this versatile dish can be served as a
light meal or added to a brunch buffet.*

Separate the fish into bite-sized pieces, certain all bones are removed, set aside. In a medium bowl, whisk eggs until frothy. Add remaining ingredients, gently stirring in salmon last. Pour into pie shell or tart shell. Bake in a preheated oven at 350° for 40-45 minutes or until golden brown and firm to the touch.

- 1 9" pie crust
- 1 cup smoked, flaked salmon or steelhead
- 1/3 cup milk
- 4 eggs
- 1 cup cottage cheese
- 1/4 cup onion, minced
- 2 tablespoons flour
- 2 tablespoons fresh parsley
- 1 tablespoon fresh cilantro
- 1 teaspoon lemon pepper seasoning salt
- Dash of paprika
- Dash of cayenne pepper

# Smokey Potato Bake

*Easy to make ahead of time, this simple potato dish
is guaranteed to be a brunch favorite.*

- 2 cups smoked, flaked salmon
  or steelhead
- 2 eggs
- 1 cup sour cream
- 2/3 cup milk
- 1/2 teaspoon dry mustard
- 1/2 teaspoon salt
- 2 teaspoons dill weed
- 2 -3 medium russet potatoes,
  peeled and thinly sliced
- 2 cups cheese (cheddar
  or Swiss)
- 4 tablespoons butter
- Lemon pepper to taste

Separate fish into bite-sized pieces,
certain all bones are removed, set aside. In
a medium bowl, mix eggs, sour cream,
milk, dry mustard, salt and dill until
frothy. Spoon 2 tablespoons of melted
butter into a 6" x 9" casserole pan. Layer
1/2 of the potatoes in the bottom of the
pan. Sprinkle 1 cup smoked fish over the
potatoes, followed by 1 cup of the cheese.
Pour 1/2 of the milk mixture on top of the
fish. Top with remaining potatoes, 2
tablespoons of butter, fish, cheese and milk
mixture. Sprinkle the top with lemon
pepper to taste. Bake, covered, in a
preheated oven at 375° for 45 minutes,
uncover and bake an additional 10 minutes
or until lightly browned.

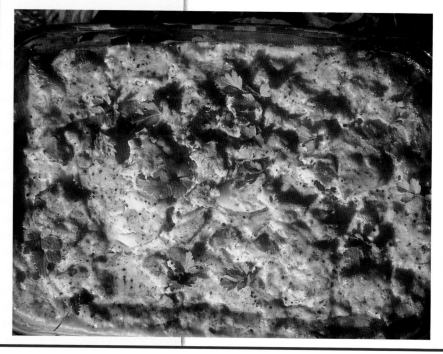

# Salmon Loaf With Honey Mustard Sauce

*The secret to an appealing salmon loaf
comes in the sauce.*

Separate fish into small pieces, certain all bones are removed. Mix salmon, beaten eggs, milk, cracker crumbs, celery, lemon juice, salt and lemon pepper in a large bowl. Lightly cover a standard-sized loaf pan with cooking spray. Spoon mixture gently into loaf pan. Bake in a preheated oven at 350° for 30 to 35 minutes or until center is set and top is golden brown.

HONEY MUSTARD SAUCE:

In a small bowl, thoroughly mix honey mustard and mayonnaise. Refrigerate until ready to serve. Double or triple the sauce if desired.

- 3 cups cooked, flaked salmon or steelhead (if using canned fish, drain)
- 3 eggs, well beaten
- 1 cup milk
- 2 1/2 cups crushed saltine cracker crumbs
- 2 stalks celery, finely chopped
- 1 tablespoon lemon juice
- 1/4 teaspoon salt
- 1/2 teaspoon lemon pepper

HONEY MUSTARD SAUCE:
- 2 tablespoons honey mustard
- 2 tablespoons mayonnaise

# Cheesy Quiche

*A versatile dish that can be served at any meal,
quiche is a quick and easy crowd pleaser.*

- 1 10" uncooked pie crust
- 2 cups cooked, flaked salmon
  or steelhead
- 6 eggs
- 2/3 cup milk
- 1/2 teaspoon onion salt
- 1/4 teaspoon black pepper
- 1/4 teaspoon paprika
- 2 tablespoons fresh,
  chopped parsley
- 1 tomato, diced
- 1/2 cup grated
  cheddar cheese
- 1/2 cup grated jack cheese

Separate fish into bite-sized pieces, certain all small bones are removed, set aside. Beat eggs, milk, salt, pepper and paprika together, set aside. Place the uncooked pie crust into a pie pan. Sprinkle flaked fish, tomato and parsley evenly in the pie shell. Sprinkle cheddar and jack cheeses over the fish. Pour the egg mixture over everything in the pie pan. Bake in a preheated oven at 350° for 35-45 minutes or until set and golden brown.

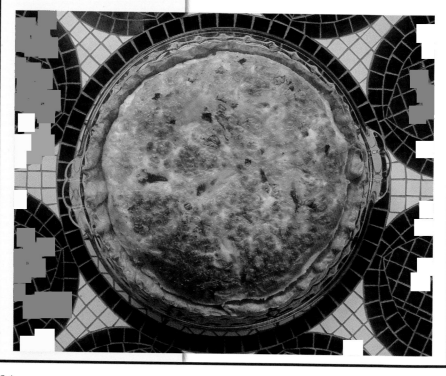

# Hearty Garden Salmon Casserole

*This is a favorite recipe of Dexter, Oregon resident, Sharon Weber, and one which receives loads of attention whenever it's cooked.*

Cook noodles according to package directions. Drain and rinse with hot water. Combine noodles with the salmon, celery, green onions and red onions. Blend in the following ingredients; sour cream, mustard, mayonnaise, thyme and salt. Put half the mixture into a lightly buttered or oiled 2-quart casserole dish. Top with half the zucchini, then repeat the layer. Sprinkle cheese on top. Bake in a preheated oven at 350° for 30 minutes. Remove from oven, check temperature (see safety tip). Add chopped tomato and serve. This dish is great with fresh sourdough bread and a garden salad.

### CONVENIENCE TIP

Make two meals at once! Depending on how many people you are feeding, you can split this recipe into two 1-quart casserole dishes or double the recipe then freeze one dish after baking. Cool the dish in the refrigerator before putting it in the freezer. Do not leave it on the counter to cool.

### SAFETY TIP

It is important that with all casseroles that have home-canned fish, to bake them at 350° making sure they have heated up to 185°. To check the temperature, insert a meat thermometer into the center of the casserole.

- 1 pint of canned salmon, drained & flaked
- 3 cups uncooked egg noodles (6 ounces)
- 1/2 cup celery, chopped
- 1/2 cup green onions, sliced
- 1/2 cup red onion, chopped
- 2/3 cup sour cream
- 2 teaspoons mustard (optional)
- 1/2 cup mayonnaise
- 1/2 teaspoon dried thyme leaves
- 1/4 to 1/2 teaspoon salt
- 1 small zucchini, washed & sliced
- 1 cup grated Monterey jack cheese
- 1 medium to large tomato, chopped

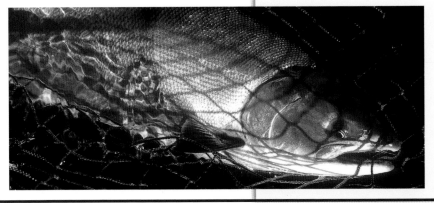

# Exotic Tastes

This is a unique section in that it captures exotic tastes from around the globe. In the process of exploring so many cultures, the authors dedicated themselves to bringing home the flavors from some of their favorite geographic locations. While such dishes involve taking a culinary risk, the special flavors that result are worth it. The ingredients for preparing these international twists are easily attained. If yearning for a change of taste, try one of these recipes.

# Cabo Fish Tacos

*One of our favorite places in Mexico is Cabo San Lucas. On our first trip there a local fishing guide insisted we try a restaurant famous for their fish tacos. Skeptical of such a combination we decided to order one to share. After our first bite, we immediately ordered more. Prepared with salmon or steelhead, they remain one of our favorite international plates.*

- 10-12 ounces, skinned, cubed, salmon or steelhead
- Juice of 1/2 of a lime
- 1 1/2 teaspoons Adobo seasoning
- 1/4 teaspoon cumin
- 1/8 teaspoon chili powder
- 3 tablespoons butter
- 8-10 taco shells

ADDITIONAL FILLINGS:

- 1 15 ounce can pinto beans
- Lettuce, shredded
- Tomatoes, chopped
- Pepper jack cheese, shredded
- Cilantro leaves
- Salsa

Skin fillets and with a pair of pliers remove any visible bones; don't worry about meat separation. Chop fish into bite-sized pieces. Spread fish in a single layer on a plate and squirt lime juice evenly over the fish. In a small bowl, mix the seasonings. Sprinkle over the fish, turning to coat all sides evenly, set aside.

Place taco shells to warm in a 200° oven. Warm beans in a small saucepan on medium to low heat. Prepare all taco fillings (lettuce, tomatoes, cilantro, cheese and salsa) prior to cooking the fish. Since the fish cooks quickly, once it is done, the meal is ready. In a medium skillet, melt butter on medium-high heat. Add fish to skillet and stir fry 3-4 minutes. Take special care not to break up the fish. Drain fish on paper towels and place in a bowl alongside other fillings. Let everyone create their own personalized tacos.

# Nori-Wrapped With Lemon Wasabi Cream

*On our many stops in Japan, we developed a liking for nori-wrapped food and the incomparable flavor of wasabi. We've found this combination goes well with salmon and steelhead, and this is Tiffany's favorite recipe in this book.*

Place fillet, skin side down, in a foil-lined baking pan. Mix sesame oil and canola oil in a small bowl. Brush oil mixture over fish. Place the nori on top of fish. Feel free to get creative with the pattern of the nori and how you cut it. Tuck ends of the nori underneath the skin side of the fish. Sprinkle with sea salt. Place on a preheated grill on low heat for 10-15 minutes or until fish is opaque and flakes in large chunks. Garnish with red and yellow peppers, sesame seeds and lemon wasabi cream.

### LEMON WASABI CREAM:

In a small mixing bowl, mix powdered wasabi and water to form a paste. Add cream, mayonnaise, lemon juice and soy sauce, whipping the mixture with a small whisk or fork until completely blended. Fold in fresh chives. Keep chilled until ready to serve. Serve over the nori-wrapped salmon or serve on the side as a sauce.

- 1 fillet of salmon or steelhead (3-6 servings)
- 1/2 teaspoon sesame oil
- 1 tablespoon canola oil
- 1 sheet nori, cut into strips
- Sea salt
- Red and yellow peppers for garnish
- Sesame seeds for garnish

### LEMON WASABI CREAM:
- 2 teaspoons powdered wasabi
- 2 teaspoons cold water
- 2 tablespoons heavy cream
- 2 tablespoons mayonnaise
- 1 teaspoon lemon juice
- 1 teaspoon soy sauce
- 1 tablespoon fresh chives, finely chopped

# Tuscan Pesto

*Not until visiting Sienna, Italy, did we come to appreciate just how good true pesto is. To this day, we regularly make it from scratch and eat it on a variety of dishes.*

- 1 fillet of salmon or steelhead (3-6 servings)
- 1 1/2 cups loosely packed, basil leaves
- 2 cloves garlic, minced
- 1/4 cup toasted pine nuts
- 1/2 cup grated parmesan cheese
- 1/4 cup olive oil
- Salt and pepper to taste

Place salmon in a greased baking dish. Finely chop basil in a food processor or mini-chopper. Add remaining ingredients and blend to form a paste. Cover fish with desired amount of pesto. Bake in a preheated oven at 400° 10 minutes per inch of thickness or until fish is opaque and flakes in large chunks. Garnish with pine nuts. The pesto can be doubled or tripled to use with pasta or other dishes. It freezes well for up to six months.

*When asked about our most memorable, life-changing travel experience, India tops the list. The sights, sounds and smells of this country are forever etched into our minds. Raita was one of the many side dishes we enjoyed daily during our travels throughout northern India.*

Combine spices in a small bowl. Rub into both sides of fillet. For a more intense flavor, the fillets can marinate with the spices for up to 3 hours. Heat oil on medium-high heat in a large skillet. Place fillets in skillet. Cook fish 5-6 minutes on each side until golden brown, turning only once. Serve with a generous helping of cucumber raita.

CUCUMBER RAITA:

Gently combine yogurt, tomato, cucumber, lemon juice, chives and salt in a medium-sized bowl. Heat a small frying pan to medium-high heat and lightly toast mustard seeds cooking them until they begin to pop. Top each serving of fish with raita and mustard seeds. Cucumber raita is also a wonderful accompaniment to the cold lemon poached fish on page 54.

- 1 skinned fillet of salmon or steelhead (3-6 servings)
- 1 teaspoon ground cumin
- 1 teaspoon ground coriander
- 1 teaspoon crushed fennel seeds
- 3/4 teaspoon crushed black pepper
- 3/4 teaspoon salt
- 1/2 teaspoon turmeric
- 1/2 teaspoon cinnamon
- 3 tablespoons vegetable oil

CUCUMBER RAITA:
- 1 cup plain yogurt
- 1 medium tomato, chopped
- 1 large cucumber, peeled and diced
- 3 tablespoons lemon juice concentrait or the juice of 1 lemon
- 1/4 cup finely chopped fresh chives
- 1/2 teaspoon sea salt
- 1 tablespoon mustard seeds

# *Thai Soy-Ginger*

*Living in Southeast Asia left us with a love of ginger root. No other geographic region can tantalize the taste buds with such exotic ingredients. This light, sweet sauce is mild and agreeable and can be used as a salad dressing and/or marinade.*

- 1 skinned fillet of salmon or steelhead (3-6 servings)
- 4 tablespoons olive oil
- 4 teaspoons soy sauce
- 2 teaspoons finely minced ginger
- 2 teaspoons sesame oil
- 1/4 cup finely minced onion
- 2 tablespoons rice vinegar
- 2 teaspoons honey

Place salmon fillet in a greased broiling pan or a metal baking dish (do not use a glass pan as the broiler may get too hot). Combine all of the ingredients for the sauce. Using a brush, paint the mixture onto the salmon. Broil 3-4 minutes and brush on more sauce, broil 3-4 more minutes and brush again, repeating one more time. Broiling time should not exceed 12 minutes and fish should be watched closely at all times. This sauce can be used to marinade fish for up to 6 hours, as the small portion of vinegar will not break down the flesh. If the fish is marinated, it does not need to be basted throughout the broiling process.

# Caribbean Sweet Chili Lime Steaks

*It seems no other combination goes so well with fish in the tropics. While on vacation in beautifully lush St. Thomas, we enjoyed fresh wahoo prepared this way in a cafe on the beach.*

Place fish steaks in a shallow pan. In a small bowl, mix lime juice, oil, garlic, honey, pepper flakes, herbs and Tabasco sauce. Pour marinade over steaks, turning steaks over to coat both sides. Marinate 5-10 minutes. On a well-greased, preheated grill, cook on high heat 4-5 minutes per side, baste with marinade as desired. Garnish with fresh lime slices.

- 6-8 salmon or steelhead steaks
- 1 lime, sliced
- Juice of 2 limes
- 2 tablespoon canola oil
- 3 cloves garlic, minced
- 2 tablespoons honey
- 1/2 tablespoon red pepper flakes
- Dash or more of Tabasco sauce
- 1 tablespoon fresh parsley, chopped
- 1 tablespoon fresh basil, chopped
- Salt to taste

# Fijian Fish

*While staying in a remote Fijian village, we enjoyed many fresh ocean-caught fish cooked in coconut milk. We have adapted the same technique to salmon and steelhead with great results. The smell alone of this dish will take you to the white sand beaches of this fascinating archipelago.*

- 1/2 skinned fillet of salmon or steelhead (2-3 servings)
- 1 tablespoon lime juice
- Salt and pepper to taste
- 1 13.5-ounce can coconut milk
- 1/2 medium onion
- 1 tomato
- 1/2 teaspoon paprika
- Dash of cayenne pepper or Tobasco sauce

Place fish fillet on a plate. Salt and pepper to taste and drizzle lime juice over fish, set aside. In a skillet, heat coconut milk and the onions just to the boiling point, stirring frequently. Quickly reduce to medium heat, add fish and remaining ingredients. Simmer on medium-low heat 20-30 minutes, stirring occasionally. Serve hot with a generous helping of the coconut milk.

*We're often asked what we miss most about living in Indonesia. While the friendly people and breathtaking equatorial beauty come to mind, we really miss the food. Hot, spicy and full of flavor, Indonesian food is truly special, particularly the tastes of western Sumatra. We have adapted one of our favorite sweet and sour fish recipes from that region, which we love on salmon and steelhead.*

Place clean fish fillet, skin side down, on a large piece of tin foil. Twist corners to form a tight fitting edge next to the salmon. This will keep the sweet and sour sauce from running off the fish fillet while it is marinading and/or cooking. Place oil in frying pan on medium heat. Sauté minced ginger root 30-60 seconds (just long enough to bring out the aroma). Add diced sweet red pepper and sauté until softened. Remove from heat and mix soy sauce, sugar, vinegar, ketchup and chili sauce in a separate bowl. Return ginger and red peppers to medium heat and add above ingredients. Stir until sugar is dissolved. Mix cornstarch with cold water and slowly stir into sauce. Stir constantly as the sauce will quickly thicken. Once sauce is thick, remove from heat. Pour 2/3 of the sauce over fish fillet, reserving 1/3 of sauce to use as a condiment. Fish may be refrigerated for up to 6 hours with the sauce or cooked right away. Bake in a preheated oven at 400° 10 minutes per inch of thickness or until fish is opaque and flakes in large chunks.

- 1 fillet of salmon or steelhead (3-6 servings)
- 1 1/2 tablespoons olive oil
- 1 tablespoon minced ginger root
- 1/2 cup diced sweet red pepper
- 2 tablespoons soy sauce
- 1/4 cup sugar
- 1/4 cup rice vinegar
- 1 tablespoon ketchup
- 1 tablespoon hot red chili sauce (or to taste)
- 1/3 cup cold water
- 1 tablespoon cornstarch

*While dining at a cafe near the Spanish Steps in Rome,
we were served this dish with fresh sole. We find it
equally delightful with salmon or steelhead.*

- 1 fillet of salmon or steelhead
  (3-6 servings)
- Italian seasoning
- Rind from 1 lemon
- 5-7 sun-dried tomatoes,
  sliced thinly
- Olive oil

Place fillet, skin side down, in aluminum foil. Generously sprinkle fillet with Italian seasoning and lemon rind. Gently rub seasoning and rind into fish. Add chopped sun-dried tomatoes. Drizzle fillet with olive oil. Seal in foil. Bake in a preheated oven at 400° 15-20 minutes or until fish is opaque and flakes in large chunks.

# South African Curry Steaks

*While on safari in Africa we were pleasantly surprised by the unusual tastes many of the southern countries had to offer. We originally had this recipe with crocodile, which tastes a lot like fish, but found it goes nicely with salmon or steelhead.*

Place salmon steaks on a greased broiling pan or a metal baking dish (do not use a glass pan as the broiler may get too hot). Grind or use a mortar and pestle to crush and combine the chili peppers, mustard seed and fennel. Combine with all of the remaining ingredients. Using a brush, paint mixture onto the salmon. Broil 3-4 minutes and brush on more sauce, broil 3-4 more minutes and brush again, repeating one more time. Broiling time should not exceed 12 minutes and fish should be watched closely at all times. This recipe can also be prepared on the grill. Before serving, squeeze a slice of lime over the fish to fully bring out the curry spices.

- 4-6 salmon or steelhead steaks
- 2 dry red chili peppers
- 1/2 teaspoon whole mustard seeds
- 1/2 teaspoon fennel
- 1/2 teaspoon sea salt
- 1 teaspoon coriander
- 1/2 teaspoon cumin
- 1/4 teaspoon turmeric
- 1/4 teaspoon cayenne pepper
- Black pepper to taste
- 4 tablespoons melted butter
- Lime for garnish

# Herbed Gravlax

*Being of Scandinavian descent, we felt it appropriate to include a dish passed on from our ancestors. A versatile family favorite, gravlax has come a long way from its traditional origin. The literal meaning of gravlax translates into "salmon from the grave" as it was buried as a means of preservation to be dug up and enjoyed all winter*

- 2 matching salmon or steelhead fillets (equaling 2 pounds)
- 1/4 cup pickling and canning salt
- 1/4 cup white sugar
- 1 tablespoon freshly ground black pepper
- 4 fresh dill sprigs
- 4 fresh rosemary sprigs
- 6 sprigs flat leafed parsley
- 2 sprigs fresh thyme
- 1/2 cup basil leaves
- 1 tablespoon fennel seeds
- 10 sprigs of chives

Lay one fillet, skin side down, in a glass baking dish. Sprinkle half of the salt, sugar, pepper mixture over fillet. Lay all of the herbs on top of fillet. Sprinkle the remaining salt, sugar and pepper mixture over the second fillet. Place the second fillet atop the first fillet, sandwiching the herbs between the two. Place the thicker section on top of the thinner section. Cover with plastic wrap and weigh down with a heavy object. We use a lead ingot for a weight as it fits well in the refrigerator. Turn the "fish sandwich" every 12 hours for 48 hours. After fish has cured, slice meat diagonally off skin. Serve with oil and vinegar or on crackers or bagels with cream cheese. See additional recipes using gravlax in the index.

*Fresh herbs are the key element in the flavoring of this recipe.*

*Gravlax can be created using various-sized fillets.*

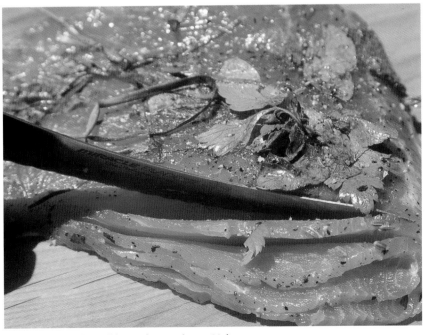

*Once covered, gravlax will keep refrigerated up to 10 days.*

# Quick & Easy Chinese

*After an enthralling evening spent watching acrobats in Beijing, we found ourselves hungry, but without our handy book of menu translations. Stepping into a lovely little restaurant we simply pointed at the fish tank and were served an elegant, lightly seasoned fish dish.*

- 1 skinned fillet of salmon or steelhead (3-6 servings)
- 1/2 cup Cantonese oyster sauce
- 1 tablespoon fresh ginger, minced
- 2 tablespoons scallions, finely sliced

Place fish fillet in a gallon-size zip-lock bag. Add remaining ingredients. Seal the bag. Squeeze bag to coat fish evenly. Cook right away or keep refrigerated until cooking time, marinating up to 2 hours. Steam, covered, on rack over rapidly boiling water 10-15 minutes or bake in a preheated oven at 400° 10 minutes per inch of thickness or until fish is opaque and flakes in large chunks. Serve with white rice.

# Marinades & Rubs

**M**arinades and rubs can be used in baking and broiling, as well as outdoor grilling and plank cooking. Fish can even be frozen in a marinade. When freezing fish in a marinade, double wrapping them in freezer paper or placing them in sealable baggies works well, to prevent loss of the marinade. For easy identification, label the fish prior to placing it in the freezer. The ease of preparing a marinade and putting it in the refrigerator or freezer until it's time to cook makes serving fish for dinner a simple, timesaving proposition.

Marinading time is dependent upon the ingredients being used and how strong a flavor you want the fish to carry. Fish soaking too long in a marinade tends to denature the proteins, resulting in a mushy texture. For this reason, some marinades with generous citric juices or vinegars should not be left for more than 30 minutes. Non-acidic marinades can soak anywhere from 30 minutes to six hours, even longer, depending on the potency of the ingredients and the overall flavor you wish to capture.

Many of the rubs can be prepared in large quantities and stored as long as there are no perishable ingredients. As with marinades, the longer a rub sits before cooking, the more intense the flavor will be. Bear in mind that fish loses its freshness quickly and it is better to preserve the quality of a fish by freezing it in the marinade or rub, versus keeping it in the refrigerator more than a few days prior to preparation.

## Marinades

## Rubs

# Orange Ginger Marinade

- 1 fillet of salmon or steelhead (3-6 servings) or 4-6 steaks
- 1 cup orange juice
- 1/4 cup teriyaki sauce
- 3"-5" fresh ginger root, sliced

Remove skin from fish fillet if desired. Place fish fillet or steaks in a gallon-size zip-lock bag. Mix marinade ingredients thoroughly in a small bowl, add to bag and seal. Squeeze bag to coat fish evenly. Keep refrigerated until cooking time. Turn over the bag every 15 minutes or so, depending on marinating time. Marinate up to 2 hours.

# Honey Dijon Marinade

Remove skin from fish fillet if desired. Place fish fillet or steaks in a gallon-size zip-lock bag. Mix the marinade ingredients thoroughly in a small bowl, add to the bag and seal. Squeeze bag to coat fish evenly. Keep refrigerated until cooking time. Turn over the bag every 30 minutes to 2 hours, depending on marinating time. Marinate up to 6 hours.

- 1 fillet of salmon or steelhead (3-6 servings)
- 1/4 cup dijon mustard
- 2 tablespoons rum
- 3 tablespoons honey

# White Wine Marinade

- 1 fillet of salmon or steelhead (3-6 servings) or 4-6 steaks
- 1/2 cup white wine
- 1 tablespoon dill
- 2 teaspoons onion powder
- 2 tablespoons olive oil
- 4 cloves garlic, minced
- 3 tablespoons soy sauce
- Lemon pepper to taste
- Salt to taste

Remove skin from fish fillet if desired. Place fish fillet or steaks in a gallon-size zip-lock bag. Mix the marinade ingredients thoroughly in a small bowl, add to the bag and seal. Squeeze bag to coat fish evenly. Keep refrigerated until cooking time. Turn over the bag every 30 minutes to 2 hours, depending on marinating time. Marinate up to 3 hours.

# Maple Butter Marinade

- 1 fillet of salmon or steelhead (3-6 servings) or 4-6 steaks
- 1/4 cup maple syrup
- 1/4 cup melted butter
- 1/4 cup onion, finely chopped
- 1/2 teaspoon cayenne pepper

Remove skin from fish fillet if desired. Place fish fillet or steaks in a gallon-size zip-lock bag. Mix the marinade ingredients thoroughly in a small bowl, add to bag and seal. Squeeze bag to coat fish evenly. Keep refrigerated until cooking time. Turn over the bag every 30 minutes to 2 hours, depending on marinating time. Marinate up to 6 hours.

Remove skin from fish fillet if desired. Place fish fillet or steaks in a gallon-size zip-lock bag. Add the remaining ingredients to the bag, placing evenly over the fish. Seal the bag. Keep refrigerated until cooking time. Turn over the bag every 10-15 minutes, depending on marinating time. Marinate up to 1 hour.

- 1 fillet of salmon or steelhead (3-6 servings) or 4-6 steaks
- 2 tablespoons olive oil
- 2 tablespoons minced garlic
- 1 lemon, sliced
- 1/2 cup fresh herbs (basil, sage, lemon balm, and/or parsley)
- Lemon pepper to taste
- Salt to taste

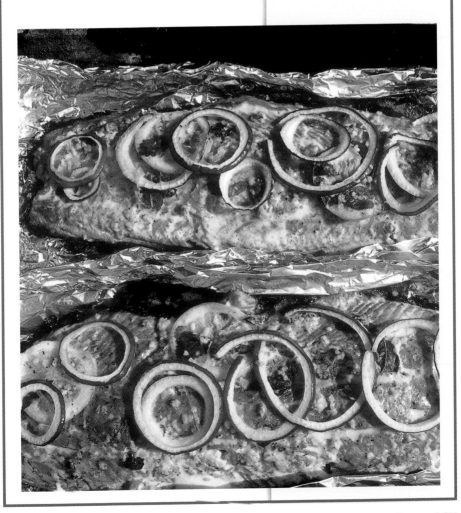

# Hot Citrus Marinade

- 1 fillet of salmon or steelhead (3-6 servings) or 4-6 steaks
- 1 lemon
- 1 lime
- 1 orange
- 1 grapefruit
- 1 tablespoon lemon juice
- 1 tablespoon lime juice
- 1/4 cup honey
- 1 teaspoon Tobasco sauce

Thinly slice the lemon, lime, orange and grapefruit. Put 1/2 of the fruits in a zip-lock bag. Placed skinned fillet or steaks on top of the fruits and cover with the additional fruits. Mix the lemon juice, lime juice, honey and Tobasco sauce in a small bowl. Pour the marinade mixture in the bag and seal. Marinade from 20 to 40 minutes, depending upon flavor desired.

Remove skin from fish fillet if desired. Place fish fillet or steaks in a gallon-size zip-lock bag. Mix the marinade ingredients thoroughly in a small bowl and add to the bag. Seal the bag. Squeeze bag to coat fish evenly. Keep refrigerated until cooking time. Turn over the bag every 10 minutes. Marinate up to 30 minutes.

- 1 fillet of salmon or steelhead (3-6 servings) or 4-6 steaks
- 2 tablespoons Miso
- 1 tablespoon honey
- 1 teaspoon sesame oil
- 1 tablespoon rice vinegar
- 1 tablespoon Sake
- 2 teaspoons lemon juice
- 2 cloves garlic
- 2" ginger root, thinly sliced

# Lime Herb Marinade

- 1 fillet of salmon or steelhead (3-6 servings) or 4-6 steaks
- 2 tablespoons olive oil
- 2 tablespoons lime juice
- 1/3 cup fresh cilantro, chopped
- 1/3 cup fresh mint, chopped
- 1 teaspoon red pepper flakes
- 1/2 teaspoon salt
- 1 lime sliced

Remove skin from fish fillet if desired. Place fish fillet or steaks in a gallon-size zip-lock bag. Add the remaining ingredients to the bag, placing evenly over the fish. Seal the bag. Keep refrigerated until cooking time. Turn over the bag every 10 minutes. Marinate up to 30 minutes.

# Italian Dressing Marinade

- 1 fillet of salmon or steelhead (3-6 servings) or 4-6 steaks
- 1 cup Italian salad dressing (any brand will work as long as it is not fat-free)

Place fish fillet or steaks in a gallon-size zip-lock bag. Pour the Italian dressing into the bag and seal. Squeeze bag to coat fish evenly. Keep refrigerated until cooking time. Turn over the bag every 30 minutes to 2 hours, depending on marinating time. Marinate up to 6 hours.

Remove skin from fish fillet if desired. Place fish fillet or steaks in a gallon-size zip-lock bag. Mix the marinade ingredients thoroughly in a small bowl and add to the bag. Seal the bag. Keep refrigerated until cooking time. Turn over the bag every 10-15 minutes, depending on marinating time. Marinate up to 2 hours.

- 1 fillet of salmon or steelhead (3-6 servings) or 4-6 steaks
- 1/3 cup white wine
- 1/4 cup canola oil
- 1 cup raspberries
- 1 teaspoon garlic salt
- 1/4 cup fresh basil leaves

# Garlic Lime Marinade

- 1 fillet of salmon or steelhead (3-6 servings) or 4-6 steaks
- 2 tablespoons lime juice
- 2 tablespoons olive oil
- 3 cloves garlic, minced
- 1 lime, thinly sliced
- Salt to taste

Remove skin from fish fillet if desired. Place fish fillet or steaks in a gallon-size zip-lock bag. Mix the marinade ingredients thoroughly in a small bowl, add to bag and seal. Squeeze bag to coat fish evenly. Keep refrigerated until cooking time. Turn over the bag every 10 minutes. Marinate up to 30 minutes.

# Smokey Marinade

Remove skin from fish fillet if desired. Place fish fillet or steaks in a gallon-size zip-lock bag. Mix the marinade ingredients thoroughly in a small bowl, add to bag and seal. Squeeze bag to coat fish evenly. Keep refrigerated until cooking time. Turn over the bag every 30 minutes to 2 hours, depending on marinating time. If preparing a large fillet, this marinade works well injected directly into the meat, but be sure to use liquid garlic. Marinate up to 6 hours.

- 1 fillet of salmon or steelhead (3-6 servings) or 4-6 steaks
- 1 tablespoon molasses
- 1 tablespoon Worcestershire sauce
- 4 cloves minced garlic or 1 teaspoon liquid garlic
- 1 teaspoon salt
- 2 tablespoons olive oil
- 1 teaspoon liquid smoke
- 1/2 teaspoon freshly ground black pepper

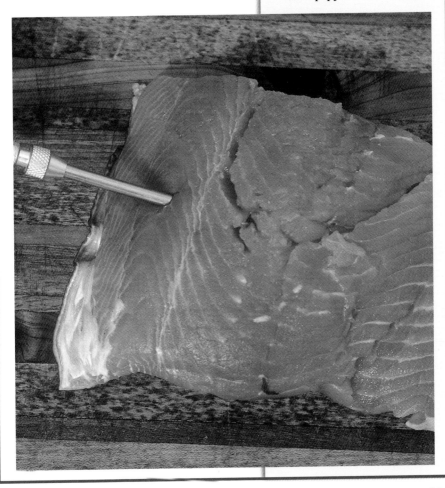

# Apricot or Plum Marinade

- 1 fillet of salmon or steelhead (3-6 servings) or 4-6 steaks
- 1/2 cup apricot syrup or 1/3 cup yellow plum jam with 1/4 cup water
- 2 tablespoons soy sauce
- 1/2 teaspoon white pepper
- 1/4 cup onion, finely chopped
- 1/2 teaspoon cinnamon

Remove skin from fish fillet if desired. Place fish fillet or steaks in a gallon-size zip-lock bag. Mix the marinade ingredients thoroughly in a small bowl, add to bag and seal. Squeeze bag to coat fish evenly. Keep refrigerated until cooking time. Turn over the bag every 30 minutes to 2 hours, depending on marinating time. Marinate up to 6 hours.

# Oil & Vinegar Marinade

- 1 fillet of salmon or steelhead (3-6 servings) or 4-6 steaks
- 1/3 cup olive oil
- 1/3 cup balsamic vinegar
- 1/3 cup lemon or lime juice
- 1/2 cup fresh parsley, chopped
- Zest from lemon or lime

Remove skin from fish fillet if desired. Place fish fillet or steaks in a gallon-size zip-lock bag. Mix the marinade ingredients thoroughly in a small bowl, add to bag and seal. Squeeze bag to coat fish evenly. Keep refrigerated until cooking time. Turn over the bag every 10 minutes. Marinate up to 30 minutes.

Thoroughly mix all ingredients in a shallow bowl. Lay steaks or fish fillet, skin side down, on a plate. Lightly score fish if thicker than 1". Gently but firmly rub ingredients into fish. This rub is a bit sticky and needs to be slowly worked into the fish. If using a skinned fillet, rub mixture on both sides. Cook immediately or for a fuller flavor let fish marinate, covered, for up to 12 hours in the refrigerator. Grill, bake, broil or pan fry as desired.

- 1 fillet of salmon or steelhead (3-6 servings) or 4-6 steaks
- 2 tablespoons brown sugar
- 2 teaspoons freshly ground black pepper
- 1 teaspoon onion powder
- 1 teaspoon garlic powder
- 1 teaspoon liquid smoke
- 1 teaspoon salt

# Spicy BBQ Rub

- 1 fillet of salmon or steelhead (3-6 servings) or 4-6 steaks
- 1 tablespoon brown sugar
- 2 teaspoons chili powder
- Rind from 1 lemon
- 1/2 teaspoon cumin
- 1/2 teaspoon salt
- 1/4 teaspoon cinnamon

Thoroughly mix all ingredients in a shallow bowl. Lay steak or fish fillet, skin side down, on a plate. Lightly score fish if thicker than 1". Gently but firmly rub ingredients into fish. If using a skinned fillet, rub mixture on both sides. Cook immediately or for a fuller flavor let fish marinate, covered, for up to 2 hours in the refrigerator. Grill, bake, broil or pan fry as desired.

Take special note of the peppers in this mix. It is advised to rub this mixture into the fish with a rinsed rubber glove. Thoroughly mix all ingredients in a shallow bowl. Lay steaks or fish fillet, skin side down, on a plate. Lightly score fish if thicker than 1". Gently but firmly rub ingredients into fish. If using a skinned fillet, rub mixture on both sides. Cook immediately or for a fuller flavor let fillet marinate, covered, for up to 2 hours in the refrigerator. Grill, bake, broil or pan fry as desired.

- 1 fillet of salmon or steelhead (3-6 servings) or 4-6 steaks
- 1 tablespoon red pepper flakes
- 1 tablespoon brown sugar
- 1 teaspoon garlic salt
- 1/4 teaspoon cayenne pepper

# Dry Herb Rub

- 1 fillet of salmon or steelhead (3-6 servings) or 4-6 steaks
- 2 bay leaves
- 2 teaspoons sugar
- 1 teaspoon basil
- 1 teaspoon thyme
- 1/2 teaspoon oregano
- 1/2 teaspoon rosemary
- 1/2 teaspoon onion powder
- 1/2 teaspoon garlic powder
- 1/2 teaspoon salt
- 1/4 teaspoon black pepper

Grind all ingredients in a food processor or using a mortar and pestle. Lay steaks or fish fillet, skin side down, on a plate. Lightly score fish if thicker than 1". Gently but firmly rub ingredients into fish. If using a skinned fillet, rub mixture on both sides. Cook immediately or for a fuller flavor let fillet marinate, covered, for up to 12 hours in the refrigerator. Grill, bake, broil or pan fry as desired.

Thoroughly mix all ingredients in a shallow bowl. Lay steaks or fish fillet, skin side down, on a plate. Lightly score fish if thicker than 1". Gently but firmly rub ingredients into the fish. If using a skinned fillet, rub mixture on both sides. Cook immediately or for a fuller flavor let fillet marinate, covered, for up to 12 hours in the refrigerator. Grill, bake, broil or pan fry as desired.

- 1 fillet of salmon or steelhead (3-6 servings) or 4-6 steaks
- 1/2 teaspoon ground cumin
- 1/2 teaspoon ground coriander
- 1/2 teaspoon crushed fennel seeds
- 1/4 teaspoon white pepper
- 1/2 teaspoon salt
- 1/4 teaspoon turmeric
- 1/4 teaspoon cinnamon
- 1/4 teaspoon cloves

# Outdoor Cooking

When it comes to cooking fish, one of the most appealing aspects is preparing it outdoors. In fact, many people choose to only cook their fish outdoors, on the grill. The grilling process can be as quick and easy or as elaborate and time-consuming as you want to make it, thus lending itself nicely to individual schedules. Be it on advanced or basic grills, or whether you use specialized equipment such as the Simple Smoker, there are many ways to expand on how you prepare fish, whereby capturing a world of new flavors.

# Tomato Rosemary

*Protected by the tomato sauce, the fillet cooks slowly over the grill in this recipe, putting forth the smooth aroma of fresh rosemary.*

- 1 skinned fillet of salmon or steelhead (3-6 servings)
- 1 8-ounce can tomato sauce
- 2 sprigs fresh rosemary
- 1 carrot, finely sliced
- 1 stalk celery, finely sliced
- 1/2 medium onion, finely sliced
- 1 teaspoon sugar
- Salt and pepper to taste

Place fillet, skin side down, on aluminum foil. Turn up the edges of the foil right next to the fish to keep any sauce from dripping onto grill. Salt and pepper fish to taste. Mix remaining ingredients and cover fillet. Place on a medium-low grill and cook 15-25 minutes, or until fish tests done. This sauce can also be put on fish prior to freezing. Place fish in freezer paper and top with the tomato sauce and vegetables. Once frozen, it can be removed from the freezer paper and placed directly on the grill. Add 10-15 minutes to grilling time for frozen fish.

*Long-time family friend, John Connolly loves fishing, and cooking his catch. This is his favorite grilling recipe, for both its ease and the enjoyment it offers.*

In a small bowl mix butter, lemon juice and seasoning salt. Baste meat side of fish. Generously spray grill with nonstick cooking spray. Heat grill to high. Place fillet, skin side down, and grill for 5 minutes. Roll fillet over onto meat side, skin should peel away as you turn the fish over. Remove the skin completely and discard any of the brown meat. Generously baste fish again, grilling 3-4 minutes. Flip back onto the original side, basting generously and cooking an additional 5-6 minutes or until fish tests done.

- 1 fillet of salmon or steelhead (3-6 servings)
- 1 cube melted butter
- Juice from 1 lemon
- Garlic seasoning salt, to taste
- Nonstick cooking spray

# *Jerry's Grilled Delight*

*Although allergic to fish of any kind, Scott's dad is an avid angler. His talents don't stop there as he is also well known for this very simple yet tasty grilling recipe.*

- 1 fillet salmon or steelhead (3-6 servings)
- 1 cup Nucoa margarine, melted
- 1 teaspoon salt or to taste
- 1/2 teaspoon pepper or to taste

Prepare fish by cutting into serving-sized portions. Mix melted margarine, salt and pepper in a basting bowl. Preheat grill on high. Generously baste flesh side of each fillet with a brush and immediately place flesh side down on grill. The objective is to quickly sear the fish and seal in juices, firming it up for easy turning. Keep grill open at all times during the preparation of this fish. Cook for approximately 2 minutes or until grill marks are apparent. Generously baste skin side of fish and immediately turn over. Grill on skin side 3-5 minutes. Repeat the margarine baste on each side 2-4 more times until fish flakes and tests done. It may take a bit longer to grill fish using this method due to the grill staying open. Remove skin from fish before serving. Lateral bones will slightly protrude from flesh, and once the fish is done can easily be plucked out, creating a boneless fillet.

*Jerry Haugen netting a spring chinook for his nephew, Craig Starmer, on Oregon's McKenzie River.*

# Dijon Rum Fish

*Long-time Alaskan resident and wild-game connoisseur, Lani Kassube, shares her favorite salmon recipe. We have enjoyed feasting on many of Lani's dishes from moose to halibut. This basic recipe is one you are sure to enjoy.*

In a small bowl mix butter, rum and brown sugar, set aside. Place fillet, skin side down, on a large sheet of aluminum foil (do not use nonstick foil or cooking spray). Paint the top of the fillet with dijon mustard and grill on medium-high heat for 5-6 minutes. It's okay if the skin starts to blacken. Remove from grill and place a sheet of foil over the mustard side of the fish. Flip the fish over and peel off the first layer of foil; the skin should stick to the foil as it's removed. Paint the rum, sugar, butter mixture over the fish. Return fish to grill on low heat for an additional 10-15 minutes or until fish tests done.

- 1 fillet of salmon or steelhead (3-6 servings)
- Dijon mustard
- 2/3 cup butter at room temperature
- 2 tablespoons rum
- 4 tablespoons brown sugar

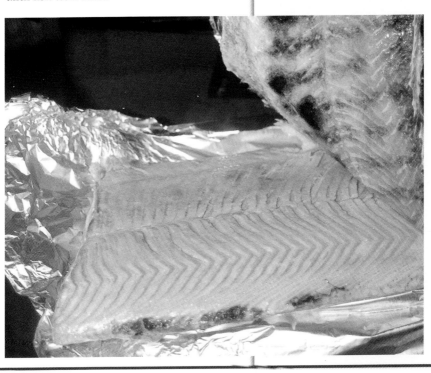

# Bob Cobb's Spicy Fish

*Another one of the Cobb family's lip-smacking recipes, it's the special spicy sauce that makes this one a hit.*

- 4 salmon or steelhead fillets (3-6 servings)
- Spicy salmon sauce (see recipe below)
- Garlic salt
- Lemon pepper

SPICY SAUCE:
- 1 teaspoon black pepper
- 2 cloves garlic, minced
- 1 teaspoon cayenne pepper
- 1/4 onion, diced
- 1 teaspoon ground mustard
- 1/4 cup red wine vinegar
- 1 teaspoon chili powder
- 1/4 cup olive oil
- 1 teaspoon paprika
- 1/4 cup butter
- 1 teaspoon Tobasco sauce
- 1 cup water
- 1 teaspoon Worcestershire sauce

Skin and score fillets. Place fillets on aluminum foil. Sprinkle with garlic salt and lemon pepper. Fold foil sides up to hold sauce, place on grill. Pour spicy sauce over fillets. Grill 15-30 minutes, depending on thickness of fillets.

SPICY SAUCE:

Mix all ingredients in small sauce pan, simmer 5 minutes.

*Bob Cobb admires a fall chinook taken on Oregon's Umpqua River.*

*A handy device, Sam's Simple Smoker is perfect for those desiring a smoke flavor in their grill. The specialized grate tool makes for easy and safe handling on virtually any grill.*

Grind all ingredients in a food processor or using a mortar and pestle. Lay fish fillet skin side down on a plate. Lightly score fish if thicker than 1". Gently but firmly rub ingredients into fish fillet. Soak 2 cups wood chips (flavor of choice) 15-20 minutes before placing in Sam's Simple Smoker. Grill 15-25 minutes, depending on thickness of the fillets.

- 1 fillet salmon or steelhead (3-6 servings)
- 2 bay leaves
- 2 teaspoons sugar
- 1 teaspoon basil
- 1 teaspoon thyme
- 1/2 teaspoon oregano
- 1/2 teaspoon rosemary
- 1/2 teaspoon onion powder
- 1/2 teaspoon garlic powder
- 1/2 teaspoon salt
- 1/4 teaspoon black pepper

*The Simple Smoker, grate tool and a wide variety of chips ideal for this style of cooking, can be obtained from www.bbqwoods.com.*

# Individual Parmesan Packets

*Easy to make ahead of time and pop on the grill, this simple recipe bursts with flavor. It is a favorite of ours served with pasta.*

- 1 fillet salmon or steelhead (3-6 servings)
- 1/2 cup butter, softened to room temperature
- 3 cloves garlic, minced
- 1/2 cup parmesan cheese
- 1 teaspoon Italian seasoning
- 8 sundried tomatoes, chopped
- Zest of 1 lemon

Divide fish into equal serving portions and place on its own square of aluminum foil. In a small bowl, mix the butter, garlic, parmesan cheese and Italian seasoning. Place a 1/4" layer on top of each fish fillet. Top with sundried tomato pieces and the lemon zest. Wrap foil loosely over fish, folding edges in (tip edges up so the butter mixture will not escape once it begins to melt). Refrigerate at least 20 minutes to firm up the butter topping on the fish. Place foil packets of fish on a preheated grill at medium heat. Grill 15-20 minutes, depending on thickness of the fillets. Open up foil packets during the last few minutes of cooking for a nicely browned top.

*Prepared ahead of time, these packets of fish can easily be cooked in camp.*

# Mike Bogue's Easy Grill

*One of the Sacramento River's premier guides, Mike Bogue of Mike Bogue's Guide Service, likes preparing his fish quick and easy. The moist, tasty results of this recipe are a Bogue family favorite.*

Lay fillet skin side down on foil. Pour desired amount of butter over fillet. Evenly distribute desired amount of garlic over fillet. Sprinkle lemon pepper over fillet. Cover with sliced onions. Loosely cover with foil, sealing edges. Place on a preheated grill. Grill on medium-low heat for 20-30 minutes or until fish tests done.

- 1 fillet salmon or steelhead (3-6 servings)
- **Melted butter**
- **Garlic**
- **Lemon pepper**
- **Sliced onions**

*Mike Bogue releasing a wild Alaskan steelhead.*

# Tiffany's Family Favorite

*Growing up, this was the way Tiffany always enjoyed salmon on the grill.*

- 1 fillet salmon or steelhead (3-6 servings)
- 1/2 cup Best Foods mayonnaise
- 1 Walla Walla onion, sliced
- Juice of 1/2 lemon
- 1 lemon, sliced
- Salt
- Lemon pepper

Place fillet, skin side down, on a large piece of aluminum foil. Squeeze 1/2 a lemon over the meat side of fillet. Salt and pepper to taste. Spread a 1/4" to 1/2" layer of mayonnaise over entire fillet. Separate onion rings and spread over fish. Top with sliced lemon and another sprinkling of lemon pepper. Fold up foil to enclose fish. If foil is not large enough, add a top sheet. Close tightly on three edges leaving the front only folded slightly so fish can easily be checked. Grill 15-25 minutes, depending on thickness of fillets. Open up foil packet during the last few minutes of cooking for a nicely browned top.

# Gesh's Kenai Cajun Fish

*Noted Alaskan Kenai River guide Brett Gesh of Alaskan Bitefinders gets client son to many monster kings each summer. Though Gesh is often pressed for time, when he has an evening to himself, this is his favorite way to prepare these fine eating fish.*

The spices in this recipe are added depending on how much flavor individuals want. Fillets can be cut ahead of time and seasoned individually, or the entire fillet can be seasoned at once. On the flesh side of the fillet, lightly sprinkle enough Cajun spice mix (Brett prefers the brand Cajun Sunshine) to turn the fillet a red color. Follow with a sprinkling of lemon pepper and a sprinkling of garlic powder. Cut the butter into equal pats and distribute evenly over fish. Grill 15-25 minutes, depending on thickness of the fillets. Serve with Spanish rice, beans and tortillas. This recipe can be baked in the oven at 350° for 20-25 minutes, or until fish tests done.

- 1 fillet of salmon or steelhead (3-6 servings)
- Cajun spice mix
- Lemon pepper
- Garlic powder
- 4-5 tablespoons butter

*Brett Gesh and his faithful dog Body with one of the world's best eating fish, a Kenai River king salmon.*

# Kebabs With Yogurt Dip

*Endless combinations of fruits and vegetables can be used with
a shish kebab. Try cherry tomatoes, peppers, mushrooms,
steamed carrots, onions or zucchini for nice color and variety.*

- 1 skinned fillet of salmon or
  steelhead (3-6 servings)
- 6 strips uncooked bacon
- 1/2 fresh pineapple, cubed
  (canned pineapple chunks
  can be used)
- 1 tablespoon lemon juice
- Salt and pepper to taste
- 5-10 wooden skewers

YOGURT DIP:
- 1 cup plain yogurt
- 1/2 clove garlic
- 4-6 fresh mint leaves
- 1 teaspoon honey
- 1 tablespoon orange juice
- 1 tablespoon finely ground
  walnuts
- 1 teaspoon lime zest

Soak wooden skewers for at least one hour prior to grilling. Cube fish and place in one layer on a plate. Drizzle lemon juice over fish and lightly salt and pepper. Leaving at least 1" at each end of the wooden skewer, put desired fruits, vegetables, bacon and fish on the skewer taking care to center the food. Grill on medium-high heat for 2-4 minutes, watching closely.

YOGURT DIP:

Mix the ingredients in a food processor. Refrigerate until ready to serve.

*There is something about cooking in cast iron that adds an old-fashioned goodness to food. This recipe is simple and a cinch to prepare on an open fire, camp stove or at home.*

In a large cast-iron skillet, melt the butter. Place fish in pan, salt and pepper to taste. Cook 5-6 minutes on each side. Try turning fish only one time to preserve fillet. Fillets should be golden brown and flake in large chunks.

- 1 skinned fillet of salmon or steelhead (3-6 servings)
- 1 cube of butter
- Salt and pepper to taste

# Stuffed Fish

*I*f you're looking to enhance the natural flavors of salmon and steelhead – while simultaneously charming the palate – try experimenting with different stuffings. A stuffed fillet is perfect for introducing variety into one's diet. The following rich fillings will make you feel as if you're dining in a five-star restaurant.

# Greek Stuffed

*Tiffany's personal favorite stuffed fish. The strong Mediterranean flavors blend beautifully and make this recipe a stand out.*

- 1 fillet of salmon or steelhead (3-6 servings)
- 3 cloves garlic, minced
- 1 tablespoon lemon juice
- 2 tablespoons whipped cream
- 1/2 cup feta cheese
- 1 teaspoon fennel seeds
- 1/2 teaspoon dried oregano
- 4-5 mint leaves, chopped
- 3 tablespoons green onion, chopped
- 1/4 cup sweet red pepper, finely chopped
- 15-20 fresh spinach leaves, chopped or torn
- 12-15 Kalamata olives, pitted and halved
- Olive oil (1/2 to 1 tablespoon)
- Sea salt

Prepare the fish fillet by cutting lengthwise through the center of fillet, leaving equal thickness on the top and bottom. Place on a large sheet of aluminum foil and set aside. Mix remaining ingredients (except the olive oil and sea salt) in a medium bowl. Place the stuffing mixture in between the cut fillet. Sprinkle sea salt atop fillet and drizzle with olive oil. Seal fish in foil and place on a preheated grill. Grill on medium-low heat for 20-30 minutes or until fish tests done. Or bake in a preheated oven at 400° 10 minutes per inch of thickness, including stuffing, or until fish is opaque and flakes in large chunks. Serve on a bed of spinach and garnish with red pepper, feta cheese, green onion and Kalamata olives if desired.

# Crab Stuffed

*The perfect end to a day spent on the ocean. Rich flavors combine to make this an exquisite meal.*

In a small skillet, melt butter on medium heat. Add garlic and onion and sauté until onions are translucent. Add crab, bread crumbs, wine and cayenne pepper. Cook on medium heat 2-3 minutes or until mixture thickens. Remove from heat and add fresh chives and parsley. Set stuffing mixture aside to cool. Prepare fish fillet by cutting lengthwise, through the center of the fillet, leaving equal thickness on the top and bottom. Place skin side down on aluminum foil. Place stuffing mixture between the cut fillet. Spread parmesan garlic butter over the top of the fillet. Loosely cover with foil, sealing edges. Place on a preheated grill. Grill on medium-low heat for 20-30 minutes or until fish tests done. Or bake in a preheated oven at 400° 10 minutes per inch of thickness, including stuffing, or until fish is opaque and flakes in large chunks. With both the grill and oven baking methods, the foil should be removed from the top for the last 5-7 minutes of cooking to brown the parmesan butter.

PARMESAN GARLIC BUTTER:
Thoroughly mix all ingredients.

- 1 fillet of salmon or steelhead (3-6 servings)
- 2 tablespoons butter
- 2 teaspoons garlic, minced
- 2 tablespoons onion, minced
- 1 cup cooked, shelled crab meat
- 1/4 cup bread crumbs
- 1/4 cup white wine
- Dash of cayenne pepper
- 2 tablespoons fresh chives, chopped
- 2 tablespoons fresh parsley, chopped
- Parmesan garlic butter for the top

PARMESAN GARLIC BUTTER:
- 1/4 cup butter, softened to room temperature
- 1-2 cloves garlic, minced
- 1/4 cup parmesan cheese
- 1/2 teaspoon Italian seasoning

# Garlic Butter Stuffed

*If you're a fan of garlic and butter, you can't go wrong
with this recipe. It's one you'll keep coming back to.*

- 1 fillet of salmon or steelhead
  (3-6 servings)
- 3 tablespoons butter
- 3 teaspoons garlic, minced
- 2 tablespoons onion, minced
- 1/4 cup bread crumbs
- 1/4 cup white wine
- Dash of cayenne pepper
- 1 tablespoon parmesan cheese
- 2 tablespoons fresh chives,
  chopped
- 2 tablespoons fresh parsley,
  chopped
- Parmesan garlic butter for
  the top (see recipe page 137)

In a small skillet, melt butter on medium heat. Add garlic and onion and sauté until onions are translucent. Add bread crumbs, wine and cayenne pepper. Cook on medium heat 2-3 minutes or until mixture thickens. Remove from heat and add fresh chives, parsley and parmesan cheese. Set stuffing mixture aside to cool. Prepare fish fillet by cutting lengthwise through the center, leaving equal thickness on top and bottom. Place skin side down on aluminum foil. Place stuffing mixture in between the cut fillet. Spread parmesan garlic butter over the top of the fillet. Seal fish in foil and place on a preheated grill. Grill on medium-low heat for 20-30 minutes or until fish tests done. Or bake in a preheated oven at 400° 10 minutes per inch of thickness, including stuffing, or until fish is opaque and flakes in large chunks. With both the grill and oven baking methods, the foil should be removed from the top for the last 5-7 minutes of cooking to brown the parmesan butter.

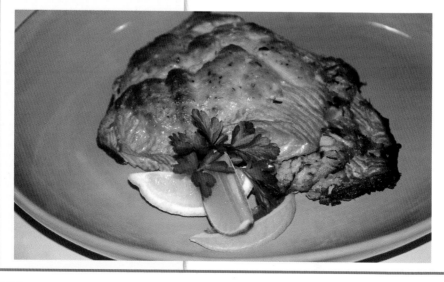

*We have actually caught people trying to sneak the stuffing out of their neighbor's fish in this recipe. Unused stuffing can be heated and used as a chip dip.*

Prepare fish fillet by cutting lengthwise through the center of the fillet leaving equal thickness on top and bottom. Place on a large sheet of aluminum foil and set aside. Mix remaining ingredients in a medium bowl. Place stuffing mixture in between the cut fillet. Seal fish in foil and place on a preheated grill. Grill on medium-low heat for 20-30 minutes or until fish tests done. Or bake in a preheated oven at 400° 10 minutes per inch of thickness, including stuffing, or until fish is opaque and flakes in large chunks.

- 1 fillet salmon or steelhead (3-6 servings)
- 1/3 cup mayonnaise
- 1/3 cup parmesan cheese
- 1/3 cup black olives, sliced
- 1 1/2 tablespoons canned mild green chilies, diced
- 1/2 cup Monterey jack cheese
- 1 6.5-ounce jar marinated artichokes

# Denise's Vegetable Stuffed

*Close friends since the 7th grade, Denise Henderson and Tiffany have shared many adventures in the kitchen together. This recipe is one Denise developed, and a favorite of her family.*

- 1 fillet salmon or steelhead (3-6 servings)
- 1/2 cup butter
- 1 teaspoon garlic powder
- 1 cup summer squash, diced
- 1 cup mushrooms, sliced
- 1 cup spinach
- Hollandaise sauce, packaged or home made
- 1 tablespoon chopped chives

HOLLANDAISE SAUCE:
- 2 teaspoons lemon juice
- 2 egg yolks
- 1/3 cup chilled butter, cut into pats

Prepare fish fillet by cutting lengthwise through the center of fillet leaving equal thickness on top and bottom. Place on a large sheet of aluminum foil and set aside. Melt butter in microwave or in a small sauce pan. Mix garlic powder into melted butter. Place vegetables in a medium mixing bowl. Pour melted garlic butter over the vegetables and toss lightly. Open fillet and fill with the buttered vegetables. Close the fillet. Seal fish in foil and place on a preheated grill. Grill on medium-low heat for 20-30 minutes or until fish tests done. Or bake in a preheated oven at 400° 10 minutes per inch of thickness, including stuffing, or until fish is opaque and flakes in large chunks. Top with hollandaise sauce and chopped chives.

HOLLANDAISE SAUCE:

In a small sauce pan, whisk lemon juice and egg yolks. Add butter and place on low heat. Stir continuously with the whisk until butter is thoroughly melted.

*Sautéed peppers, onions and tomatoes always bring back
fond memories of the fresh vegetables Tiffany enjoyed daily
while living on the Costa Del Sol in Spain.*

Prepare fish fillet by cutting lengthwise through the center of fillet leaving equal thickness on top and bottom. Place on a large sheet of aluminum foil, turn the edges up to catch the marinade. In a small bowl, mix lime juice and sesame oil. Open fillet and pour 1/2 of the lime juice and sesame oil mixture over fillet. Close fillet and pour the remaining marinade over top. Place in the refrigerator 10-20 minutes. In a medium skillet, sauté the peppers and onion until soft. Add tomatoes and sesame seeds and sauté an additional 5 minutes on medium-low heat. Remove marinated fish from the refrigerator. Open up the fillet, spread the sautéed vegetable mixture (leaving approximately 1 cup of the mixture in the skillet) inside the fish and close. Lightly salt and pepper top of the fillet. Seal fish in foil and place on a preheated grill. While the fish is cooking, keep the reserved vegetable mixture warm. Grill on medium-low heat for 20-30 minutes or until fish tests done. Or bake in a preheated oven at 400° 10 minutes per inch of thickness, including stuffing, or until fish is opaque and flakes in large chunks. Top with cooked vegetable mixture, fresh parsley and garnish with a wedge of lime.

- 1 fillet of salmon or steelhead (3-6 servings)
- 1 tablespoon sesame oil
- 2 tablespoons lime juice
- 1 tablespoon canola oil
- 1 red pepper, diced
- 1 yellow pepper, diced
- 1/2 medium sweet onion, diced
- 1 tomato, diced
- 1/4 cup toasted sesame seeds
- Salt and pepper to taste
- Parsley, for garnish
- Lime wedges, for garnish

# Roasted Pepper Stuffed

*The peppers in this recipe can be roasted from scratch but we prefer using store-bought marinated in olive oil.*

- 1 fillet salmon or steelhead (3-6 servings)
- 1 cup roasted red and yellow sweet peppers
- 10 sundried tomatoes
- 1/3 cup basil leaves
- 2 tablespoons olive oil
- Salt to taste

Prepare fish fillet by cutting lengthwise through the center of fillet leaving equal thickness on top and bottom. Place on a large sheet of aluminum foil. Open up fillet and lightly salt. Evenly distribute peppers, tomatoes and cleaned basil leaves inside the fish. Drizzle with 1 tablespoon olive oil. Close the fillet. Lightly salt top of fillet and drizzle with the remaining 1 tablespoon olive oil. Seal fish in foil and place on a preheated grill. Grill on medium-low heat for 20-30 minutes or until fish tests done. Or bake in a preheated oven at 400° 10 minutes per inch of thickness, including stuffing, or until fish is opaque and flakes in large chunks.

*Rosemary is a fragrant herb, it's nice having a vase of it in the kitchen. Ancient Greeks actually believed it improved their memory; we like the aroma and flavor it offers fish.*

Prepare fish fillet by cutting lengthwise through the center of fillet leaving equal thickness on top and bottom. Place on a large sheet of aluminum foil. Sprinkle fillet on top and inside lightly with salt and pepper. Open up fillet, spread garlic evenly over fish. Place rosemary sprigs and sliced lemons evenly on one side of the open fish. Distribute 4-5 butter pats over the rosemary and lemons and close up fish. Distribute remaining pats of butter atop closed fillet. Seal fish in foil and place on a preheated grill. Grill on medium-low heat for 20-30 minutes or until fish tests done. Or bake in a preheated oven at 400° 10 minutes per inch of thickness, including stuffing, or until fish is opaque and flakes in large chunks.

- 1 fillet salmon or steelhead (3-6 servings)
- 4 cloves garlic, minced
- 4-6 sprigs fresh rosemary
- 2 lemons sliced
- 6 tablespoons chilled butter, cut into 8-10 thin slices
- Salt and pepper to taste

# Wild Rice Stuffed

*To quickly prepare this dish, use a prepackaged wild rice adding fresh herbs, extra butter and garlic.*

- Whole salmon or steelhead, cleaned with tail and head removed
- Your favorite wild rice mix
- 1/2 cup mixed fresh herbs (parsley, basil, dill, chives, lemon balm, thyme)
- 1/4 cup butter
- 2 cloves garlic, minced
- 1/2 onion, sliced
- 1/2 cup parsley, chopped
- Salt and pepper to taste

Prepare wild rice as directed on package. Adding extra butter and garlic with the water, toss in the fresh herbs once the rice is cooked. Place fish on a large piece of aluminum foil. Lightly salt and pepper the body cavity. Put as much of the rice mixture in the fish as possible. Any leftover mix can be served along with the fish, but take special care not to touch the prepared rice you will be eating separately with any of the raw fish or the utensils used in stuffing the fish. Cover the fish with sliced onions and parsley. Seal fish in a double layer of foil and place on a preheated grill. Grill on medium heat for 20 minutes on each side.

# Herb Stuffed

*A fun way to cook fresh-caught fish in a campfire, over the coals or on the grill. All you need is a handful of herbs to assemble this tasty meal.*

Place fish on a large piece of aluminum foil. Lightly salt and pepper the body cavity. Stuff as many of the herbs as possible into the body cavity. Save a few sprigs of each herb to use as garnish after cooking. Seal fish in a double layer of foil and place on a preheated grill. Grill on medium heat for 15 minutes on each side.

- 1 whole salmon or steelhead (8-9 pounds), cleaned with tail and head intact
- 1 bunch parsley
- 1 bunch dill
- 1 cup basil
- 2 stalks celery
- Salt and pepper to taste

# Plank Cooking

Though a relatively new concept among many backyard chefs, cooking fish on a plank has a rich history. This style of cooking affords great flexibility, be it on the grill or in the home. While preparing planked fish on a barbecue is the most common means, cooking fish on a plank can also be accomplished in the oven. For added flavor, planks can be soaked in apple juice or wine to create a special essence. When done, the fish can be served directly on the plank, making for great dinner conversation.

Planks can be acquired, ready to use, at many places, including specialty companies like bbqwoods.com. You may also choose woods from the local lumber yard or building supply store, or you can chop and dry it yourself. Be certain the woods purchased are raw and untreated. Planks ranging from 1/2 to 1 inch in thickness are best, with the length best determined by the size fillets you wish to cook. Cedar, alder, cherry, oak, hickory and maple are some of the ideal planking woods.

If new to plank cooking, trial and error is the best way to truly learn the potential of this approach, for so much depends on personal preference when trying to achieve a desired smoke flavor. For those craving a heavy smoke flavor, let the plank catch on fire for a brief moment, then douse with a spray bottle. The extra smoke produced after extinguishing the flame will enhance the end result. If you want to extend the life of a plank for repeated use, or if only a mild wood flavor is desired, take care not to let the fire overchar the plank.

Fish cooked on a plank takes about the same time to prepare as on an exposed grill, maybe a bit longer depending on thickness. For added flavor, keep grill covered, allowing the fish to absorb the lingering smoke while simmering. Many fish aficionados claim there's no better way to attain a moist, flavor-packed salmon or steelhead than cooking on a plank.

# Cherry Lemon Planked

*A simple planking recipe, the mild cherry wood is
picked up throughout the fish, and the lemons keep
it tender and moist.*

- 1 fillet of salmon or steelhead
  (3-6 servings)
- Salt
- Lemon pepper
- 1 lemon thinly sliced
- 1/4 cup fresh chives, finely
  chopped
- Olive oil
- 1 lemon for garnish (optional)
- 1 cherry wood plank

Prepare the cherry wood plank by fully submerging it in water for 1 hour. Dry the plank in a 350° oven for 10 minutes or place in the middle of a grill that has been preheated to high heat for 5 minutes. Rub both sides of the plank with olive oil.

Place salmon fillet, skin side down, on the plank. Salt and lemon pepper the fish to taste. Sprinkle chives over the fillet. Place lemon wedges evenly over fish. Place on a hot grill and turn gas to medium heat. Cook for 10 minutes trying not to lift the lid (if worried about flare ups, check, but realize that flare ups may be worse when opening the lid). Any time you open the grill, be prepared with a squirt bottle of water and douse any part of the plank that is on fire. It is good to have a bit of fire since once you spray it with water it will really start to smoke. Turn the gas grill to low heat for an additional 10-15 minutes depending on the thickness of the fish. The plank may be charred and the lemons blackened, but once you remove the fish from the plank, and the lemons from the fish, you have a juicy, delectable meal. Garnish with fresh sliced lemons if desired.

# Marinated Onion Maple Planked

*You don't have to be a fan of onions to enjoy*
*this slightly sweet, moist planked fish.*

For best results, marinate the onions overnight. Thinly slice onion and place in a large zip-lock bag. Add the oil, vinegar, Worcestershire sauce, maple syrup, salt and pepper. Mix by hand. Seal the bag and refrigerate overnight or up to 24 hours. Prepare the maple wood plank by fully submerging it in apple juice. Water can be used but the apple juice imparts a sweeter smoke flavor (soaking at least one hour). Dry the plank in a 350° oven for 10 minutes. Place 1/3 of the marinated onions on the plank. Place the fish, skin side down, over the onions. Lightly salt and pepper the fish if desired then put remaining onions over the fillet. Completely cover the fillet. Place on a hot grill and turn gas to medium heat. Cook for 10 minutes trying not to lift the lid if possible (if worried about flare ups, check but realize that flare ups may be worse when opening the lid). Any time you open the grill, be prepared with a squirt bottle of water and douse any part of the plank that is on fire. It is good to have a bit of fire since once you spray it with water it will really start to smoke. Turn the gas grill to low heat for an additional 10-15 minutes depending on the thickness of the fish. If the onions are charred during the cooking process, remove before serving.

- 1 fillet of salmon or steelhead (3-6 servings)
- 1 large Walla Walla onion (or onion of your choice)
- 1/4 cup oil
- 2 tablespoons vinegar
- 2 tablespoons Worcestershire sauce
- 2 tablespoons real maple syrup
- 1 teaspoon salt
- 1/2 teaspoon black pepper
- 6-8 cups apple juice
- 1 maple wood plank

# Cedar-Planked Citrus Salmon

*Dave Prindel is a lifelong angler and devoted science teacher who does all he can to convey the value of the outdoors to the younger generation. He's also a great cook, and this is his favorite planking recipe, one that receives all the attention, no matter how many dishes may appear at a potluck.*

- 1 whole salmon or steelhead, cut into 2 fillets
- 1/2 cup butter
- 1-2 Mayan onions, sliced
- 1/4 cup brown sugar
- 1 orange, peeled and sliced 1/8"
- 1 lemon, peeled and sliced 1/8"
- 1 10-ounce can pineapple juice
- 1/4 cup white vinegar
- 1 cup brown sugar
- 1 tablespoon cornstarch
- 2 tablespoons soy sauce
- 1/4 cup green pepper, diced
- 1/4 cup red pepper, diced
- salt and pepper to taste
- 1 cedar plank (1" x 12" x 24")

Soak cedar plank for at least 48 hours. Remove plank from water right before baking or grilling. Place fish fillets, skin side down, on the plank. Salt and pepper fish to taste. Evenly distribute peeled and sliced orange and lemon segments over fish fillets. In a medium skillet on high heat, melt butter. Add onions and 1/4 cup brown sugar, cook until caramelized. Put caramelized onions on top of the orange and lemon segments. In a medium sauce pan on medium-high heat, combine pineapple juice, vinegar and 1 cup brown sugar. In a small bowl, mix cornstarch and soy sauce. Add to pineapple juice mixture and bring to a boil. Pour over fillets. Sprinkle green and red peppers over the top of fillets. Place on a hot grill and turn gas to medium heat. Cook for 10 minutes trying not to lift the lid if possible (if you are worried about flare ups, check but realize that the flare ups may be worse when you open the lid). Any time you open the grill, be prepared with a squirt bottle of water and douse any part of the plank that is on fire. It is good to have a bit of fire since once you spray it with water it will really start to smoke. Turn the gas grill to low heat for an additional 10-15 minutes depending on the thickness of the fish.

# Ginger Topped on Oak

*Zesty and fresh, this very simple recipe adds a
unique flavor with both the plank and
ginger tastes shining through.*

For best results, marinate the thinly sliced ginger root overnight in 1 tablespoon of olive oil. When slicing, cut across the grain to make dime to nickel size pieces that will cover the fish. The ginger does not need to be peeled. Prepare the oak wood plank by fully submerging it in water and soaking for 1 hour. Dry the plank in a 350° oven for 10 minutes or place in the middle of a grill that has been preheated to high, heat for 5 minutes. Rub both sides of the plank with olive oil. Place fish fillet skin side down on the plank. Brush the fillet with 1 teaspoon sesame oil, if you do not desire a sesame taste, substitute olive oil in this step. Salt and pepper fish to taste. Fully cover fillet with marinated ginger, overlapping ginger slices if possible. Place on a hot grill and turn gas to medium heat. Cook for 10 minutes trying not to lift the lid if possible (if worried about flare ups, check but realize that flare ups may be worse when opening the lid). Any time you open the grill, be prepared with a squirt bottle of water and douse any part of the plank that is on fire. It is good to have a bit of fire since once you spray it with water it will really start to smoke. Turn the gas grill to low heat for an additional 10-15 minutes, depending on thickness of the fish. If the ginger is charred during the cooking process, remove before serving.

- 1 fillet of salmon or steelhead (3-6 servings)
- 1 large section of ginger root, thinly sliced
- 1 teaspoon sesame oil
- 1 tablespoon olive oil
- Salt and pepper to taste
- 1 oak plank

# Smokey Rub on Alder

*Smoked-fish lovers will delight in this subtle, smokey recipe.*
*Leftovers, if there are any, work well in salads or casseroles.*

- 1 fillet of salmon or steelhead
  (3-6 servings)

SMOKEY RUB:

- 2 tablespoons brown sugar
- 2 teaspoons freshly ground
  black pepper
- 1 teaspoon onion powder
- 1 teaspoon garlic powder
- 1 teaspoon liquid smoke
- 1 teaspoon salt
- 1 alder plank

Thoroughly mix all ingredients in a shallow bowl. Lay fish fillet, skin side down, on a plate. Lightly score fish if thicker than 1". Gently but firmly rub ingredients into fish fillet. This rub is a bit sticky and needs to be slowly worked into the fish. If using a skinned fillet, rub mixture on both sides. Cook immediately or for a fuller flavor let the fillet marinate, covered, for up to 12 hours in the refrigerator. Prepare the alder wood plank by fully submerging it in water and soaking for 1 hour. Dry the plank in a 350° oven for 10 minutes or place in the middle of a grill that has been preheated to high heat for 5 minutes. Rub both sides of plank with olive oil. Place fillet, skin side down, on plank. Place on a hot grill and turn gas to medium heat. Cook for 10 minutes trying not to lift the lid (if worried about flare ups, check, but realize that flare ups may be worse when opening the lid). Any time you open the grill, be prepared with a squirt bottle of water and douse any part of the plank that is on fire. It is good to have a bit of fire since once you spray it with water it will really start to smoke. Turn the gas grill to low heat for an additional 10-15 minutes depending on the thickness of the fish. Serve right from the plank.

# McKenzie River Cedar Planked

*John Gross, of Roaring Fork Guide Service, is a longtime Willamette Valley guide who enjoys plank cooking and all it has to offer. He personally splits his cedar planks off rounds from a tree harvested on his property overlooking the world-famous McKenzie River.*

- 1 fillet salmon or steelhead (3-6 servings)
- 1 cup teriyaki or soy sauce
- 1 cup Bernstein's Italian salad dressing (do not use low fat or fat free)
- 1 tablespoon dry dill weed
- 1 teaspoon Cajun seasoning
- 1 cedar plank

Mix the above ingredients for the marinade in a shallow-sided plastic container with a lid. Place the fillet, meat side down, into the marinade. Cover and marinate in the refrigerator for at least 3 hours. A thick fillet can marinate overnight. Note, the above is a basic recipe. For folks craving a hint of sweetness, add a variety of ingredients such as maple syrup, apricot jam, pineapple juice or marmalade. All of these have been used with interesting and palatable results. Soak cedar plank in water for at least 20 minutes. Bring the grill up to a high temperature. Grease the grill and place fillet, meat side down, directly onto the grill. The objective is to sear the meat fast to hold the juices and achieve those aesthetically pleasing grill lines on the meat. Searing may take 3-8 minutes. Place cedar plank directly on the grill. Flip the fillet, skin side down, onto the cedar plank. Brush the fillet with a coating of marinade as a baste. Cover the grill for 15-25 minutes. After a few minutes the bottom of your cedar plank will catch on fire. This is good. Do not put out the fire. The smoke from the plank will swirl around in the covered barbecue producing the delicate yet aromatic flavor we are after. During the cooking process, baste the fish at least 3 or 4 times to keep it moist and to monitor cooking. Baste quickly so as to maximize use of tasty smoke. Always recover the barbecue between bastings. For an interesting twist, folks with an adventuresome palate have been known to add a little grated ginger root and some orange slices on top the filet during the final 10 minutes of the planking process.

*John Gross prefers chopping his own planks on which to cook.*

# Costa Rican Style

*Another favorite recipe John Gross developed for his sister who follows a low-sodium diet. He became acquainted with these seasonings while serving in the Peace Corps, which took him to some interesting parts of the world.*

- 1 fillet of salmon or steelhead (2-4 servings)
- 1/2 cup fresh squeezed lemon juice
- 1/4 cup olive oil
- 1 teaspoon minced garlic
- 1/2 handful of coarsely chopped fresh cilantro
- 1 cedar plank

Marinate fish in the above ingredients up to 30 minutes. Follow plank grilling directions in recipe on page 153.

# Cabbage-Wrapped on Hickory

*Unbelievably tender, this method nicely
protects the fish fillet from any charring.*

Prepare hickory wood plank by fully submerging it in water and soaking for 1 hour. Dry plank in a 350° oven for 10 minutes or place in the middle of a grill that has been preheated to high heat for 5 minutes. Rub both sides of plank with olive oil. Place 2-3 cabbage leaves on the prepared plank. Lay fish fillet on top of the cabbage, skin side down. Salt and lemon pepper fish to taste. Place lemon slices atop fish and drizzle the olive oil over lemons. Wrap remaining leaves around fillet, tucking under both sides of fish. Repeat with another layer on top going in the opposite direction. Thread a presoaked (at least 1 hour in water) wooden skewer through the top layer of the cabbage leaves to keep them fastened together. Place on a hot grill and turn gas to medium heat. Cook for 10 minutes trying not to lift the lid (if worried about flare ups, check, but realize that flare ups may be worse when opening the lid). Any time you open the grill, be prepared with a squirt bottle of water and douse any part of the plank that is on fire. It is good to have a bit of fire since once you spray it with water the plank will really start to smoke. Turn the gas grill to low heat for an additional 10-15 minutes, depending on thickness of fish. The plank may be charred and the cabbage scorched, but once you remove the fish from the plank and the cabbage leaves, you have a juicy, delectable piece of fish.

- 1 fillet of salmon or steelhead (3-6 servings)
- 8-10 Chinese cabbage leaves
- Lemon pepper to taste
- Salt to taste
- 1/2 tablespoon olive oil, optional
- Wooden skewer
- Lemon slices
- 1 hickory plank

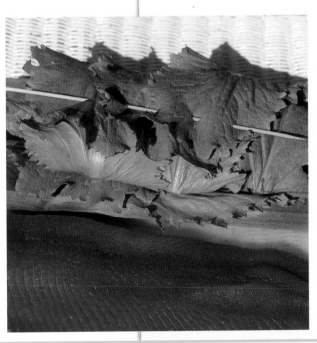

# Fresh Herbs on Oak

*Depending on the season and availability of some herbs, this recipe seems to come out differently each time we prepare it. Try it with one or two of your favorite flavors.*

- 1 fillet salmon or steelhead (3-6 servings)
- Salt and pepper to taste
- Olive oil
- Assortment of at least 3 fresh herbs of choice, including but not limited to:
  Tarragon
  Parsley
  Basil
  Lemon balm
  Summer savory
  Thyme
  Chives
- 1 oak plank

Prepare oak wood plank by fully submerging it in water and soaking for 1 hour. Dry the plank in a 350° oven for 10 minutes or place in the middle of a grill that has been preheated to high heat for 5 minutes. Rub both sides of the plank with olive oil. Divide desired herbs into two equal portions. Lay one bunch of herbs on the plank. Lay the fish, skin side down. Salt and pepper the fillet. Drizzle olive oil over the fillet and top with remaining herbs. Place on a hot grill and turn gas to medium heat. Cook for 10 minutes trying not to lift the lid (if worried about flare ups, check, but realize that flare ups may be worse when opening the lid). Any time you open the grill, be prepared with a squirt bottle of water and douse any part of the plank that is on fire. It is good to have a bit of fire since once you spray it with water the plank will really start to smoke. Turn the gas grill to low heat for an additional 10-15 minutes depending on thickness of the fish. The plank may be charred and some of the herbs scorched, but once you remove the fish from the plank, you have a moist, flavorsome piece of fish. Garnish with additional fresh herbs if desired.

# Honey Lime Oven Cedar Planked

*Too cold to fire up the grill? The hearty smoked flavor of
a planked fish can be created in the oven too.*

Marinate fillet in Worcestershire sauce for up to one hour prior to cooking. To speed up the marinating process the fillet can be injected with the sauce and cooked immediately. Prepare the cedar wood plank by fully submerging it in water and soaking for 1 hour. Dry the plank in a 350° oven for 10 minutes. Place the plank in a baking pan and lay out the slices from one of the limes. Place the fillet, skin side down, on the lime slices. In a small bowl, mix honey, garlic and butter. Spread butter mixture evenly over fish. Place the slices from the other lime atop the butter mixture. Pour a few cups of water into the baking pan. Do not let the water reach the top of the plank, you do not want the fish to come into contact with the water. Place in a 350° oven and bake 15-25 minutes, depending on thickness of the fillet. If evaporation occurs during cooking, add more water.

- 1 fillet salmon or steelhead (3-6 servings)
- 2 tablespoons Worcestershire sauce
- 2 limes, thinly sliced
- 1 tablespoon honey
- 2 cloves garlic, minced
- 2 tablespoons softened butter
- 1 cedar plank

# Miso-Glazed Steaks on Oak

*Another method of planking in the oven, soaking the oak plank in red wine prior to baking infuses the wood with a richer flavor.*

- 2-4 salmon or steelhead steaks, cut to desired thickness
- 1 tablespoon honey
- 2 tablespoons white miso
- 2 tablespoons canola oil
- 1 tablespoon rice wine vinegar
- 1 clove garlic, minced
- 4 cups red wine
- 1 oak plank

Prepare oak wood plank by fully submerging it in red wine and soaking for at least 1 hour and up to 24 hours. Dry plank in a 350° oven for 10 minutes. In a small bowl, mix honey, miso, oil, vinegar and garlic until thoroughly blended. Baste each side of the steaks with glaze and place on the hot plank. Place plank directly on oven rack. Put a foil- lined baking pan on the rack beneath the plank to catch any glaze drippings. Bake in a preheated 350° oven for 15-25 minutes, depending upon thickness of the steaks. Baste every 5-7 minutes, turning steaks once.

# Wine Selection

When it comes to selecting wines for salmon and steelhead, what one desires is based on personal preference. As a general rule, red wines typically complement red meats while white wines go nicely with white meat and flakey fish. Because salmon and steelhead fall between the heavier red meats and lighter white-fleshed fish, there is more flexibility when it comes to selecting the proper wine.

In general, Pinot Noir is a good, overall selection to serve with fish. Noir is a lighter red wine, offering a fruitier taste which nicely accentuates the oils present in salmon and steelhead.

However, when serving spicy fish, be careful with red wines, as they can accentuate the hotness left behind by the fish. When spicy fish is on the menu, white wine may be a more comfortable selection. For this purpose, Sauvignon Blanc is excellent, and Pinot Gris is a good choice as well. These white wines are more friendly with spicy fish, helping to cool the palate.

With some of the more exotic dishes, those with a strong international flavor, Chardonnay is a good choice. Though Chardonnay can be overpowering at times, it's good for offsetting the spicy flavors carried in some of these recipes. At the same time, the buttery flavor of Chardonnay nicely complements fish prepared in a cream sauce, as well as fish stuffed with vegetables.

When it comes to selecting wines for fish that has been grilled, planked or carries a smoke flavoring, Cabernet Sauvignon is nice. This is a heavier red wine, usually intended for meatier dishes. However, you'll discover this wine also blends well with these robust recipes.

Fish appetizers are popular, and selecting a wine for this largely depends on each individual's personal preference, seeing as how it's served before the main course. A good choice here is a Sauvignon Blanc, as it's light, dry and fruity with a bit of a grassy, lemon flavor. The refreshing flavor of a Blanc also makes it ideal for serving with salmon salads. Then again, a Cabernet fits nicely with a salad, too. If having a large dinner party, you may elect to serve both wines, quenching the desires of both the red- and white-wine lovers.

When choosing a wine to serve with salmon or steelhead, it's hard to go wrong. Though appeasing your own desire is simple, based on the fact you know what your palate prefers, satisfying the needs of others is also easy, especially when adhering to the general guidelines offered here.

# Preparation

More than any other aspect touched on in this book, the quality of the cooked fish that ends up on your platter is most influenced by how well the fish is cared for once caught. No matter which recipe you use, how long the fish may have soaked in a marinade or what magic was pulled-off during the cooking process, the final outcome will only be as good as the care that went into the fish, and it begins the moment a fish is landed.

The following sections deal with the proper care and handling of fish, offering sound advice based on years of personal experience and experimentation. We will address the cleaning and cooling stages of meat care, meat-cutting techniques and storage and preservation. Though these methods are applied in some form by every angler, it's often done in haste or without regard to the biological factors impacting a dead fish.

Some practices may be old habits that are hard to break, but they can be easily remedied to yield better-tasting meat. For example, many anglers, upon catching a fish, kill it and throw it in a fish box. The meat will be far better tasting if that same fish is killed, bled, disemboweled and placed on ice. The added steps take little extra effort, and the quality of meat will be noticed in the first bite you sink your teeth into.

By taking measures to properly handle fish – from the time they are caught to the time they go into the freezer – a tastier, more satisfying end product will be the result. Though some of these steps require a bit more time than perhaps you're used to, there's no denying the marked difference that will be noticed in the quality of the fish as it passes your lips. You've gone to the effort of attaining your fish, now help accentuate its true flavor to the fullest potential.

# Cleaning & Cooling

*Bleeding a fish soon after it's caught inhibits bacterial growth and ensures a better-tasting product.*

Salmon and steelhead are big fish. When fishing on a river, unlike with trout, avoid placing them on a stringer in an attempt to keep them alive. The stress brought on by such action causes an increased buildup of lactic acid within the fish, noticeably tainting the overall quality of the meat. In addition, the surface temperature of many rivers from which spring chinook and summer steelhead are taken are so high, the fish actually begins cooking in its own skin. The end result is a soft- textured, strong-tasting fish that will likely taint the palate of anyone who eats it.

When pursuing these fish in rivers, deliver a quick blow to the top of the head, right between and just back from the eyes. If fishing from a boat, it's best to deliver the death blow while the fish is in the net, over the water. Bringing live fish in the boat results in uncontrolled flailing about, and bruised flesh carries a strong taste due to the high blood content.

Before putting the fish in a cooler and making another cast, sever a gill so the fish will bleed out. Blood coagulates rapidly in dead fish, and becomes a hotbed for bacteria. The more blood that's present in a fish, the more potential for bacteria to thrive, thus fouling the taste. By bleeding a fish as soon as possible after being caught, the quality of meat dramatically increases.

If possible, it's even better to clean the fish, removing the entrails and gills. This assures that no stomach acids, digestive enzymes, tissue-destroying bacteria or excess blood will leech into the meat, otherwise denigrating its value. Anglers should note, some states do not allow fish entrails to be discarded into a stream, but this doesn't mean you can't clean your fish on the river. Simply take a bag or bucket to put the entrails into, disposing of the waste when you get home.

In ocean-caught fish, it's ideal to have the entrails fully removed within five minutes of being caught. This is because these voracious predators are aggressively feeding while at sea, and to accommodate the amount of prey they ingest, a heightened level of digestive enzymes are produced. Even when dead, these enzymes are at work inside the fish, digesting the membrane that separates the meat from the gut cavity and even the meat itself. By quickly removing the internal organs in any fish, the overall quality of the meat improves.

No matter where you are – in the ocean, on a river, in a boat or on the bank – it's best to get your fish on ice as quickly as possible. The sooner the meat can be cooled, the more firm and better tasting the flesh will be. During late fall and winter months, the air temperature is often cool enough to keep a fish until you've reached home. On hot summer days, it's best to have a cooler of ice handy. If bank fishing a river in the summer, it's not usually feasible to tote a bulky cooler filled with ice. In this case, clean the fish and hang it in a shady place. Find the coolest, darkest place to hang the fish, making sure direct sunlight does not strike the carcass during the course of the day.

If fishing from a boat, be it at sea or on a river, having a cooler of ice is preferred over tossing the fish into a metal box. Crushed ice is best, as it molds around the body of the fish, quickly cooling it. Ice cubes from the freezer also work, and can be stockpiled in a larger freezer days prior to hitting the water.

Once a fish is caught, break open a few bags of ice and surround the fish with it. To properly cool a fish, it's best if it can be gutted and the cavity packed with ice. Fish packed in ice within a good, airtight cooler can be kept for days. Be sure to open the bottom spigot to let the melted water drain, adding fresh ice as needed. Prior to placing the fish on ice or in the refrigerator, rinse thoroughly with cool tap water; this can remove up to 90% of the bacteria on the surface of the fish.

In our large Coleman coolers, we've kept multiple fillets up to five days, something that's handy if desiring to cook fish fresh, or while gathering ingredients to create a special marinade prior to placing the fish in the freezer. When keeping fresh fish this long, add ice daily, making certain all fillets are surrounded by ice. Store-bought fish should be cooked within one or two days, or if keeping for the long term, should immediately be placed in the freezer. Remember, the ultimate goal is to achieve the best tasting meat, and this can only be done by cooling the fish as soon as possible after it's been caught.

*Placing fish on ice, especially on hot days, is essential in preserving and maintaining the quality of the meat.*

# Scaling Your Catch

P rior to the long-term storage or cooking of any whole fish, fillets or steaks, should first be scaled. Fish carry a great deal of slime, which is especially true the further it moves up river from the ocean. Like the gills, slime is high in spoilage bacteria and these quickly multiply once a fish has died. By ridding the body of its scales and slime, the meat is less likely to be ruined by these spoilers. Slime also picks up any dirt and nasty residues it comes in contact with, another reason to remove the scales. If an unscaled fish comes in contact with meat, something that's inevitable no matter how careful you are, not only will a degree of spoilage occur, but a strong fish taste is typically transferred to the flesh.

*The scales of ocean-caught fish can be removed simply with a hose.*

Ocean-caught fish are easy to scale, and can be done with a regular garden hose. Cleaning stations at boat launches or situated around local marinas often have a hose present, making for easy work. Simply lay the fish on one side, tail facing you, and give it a blast with a high-power stream of water from tail to head, against the scales. Flip the fish over and repeat. In seconds the fish is free of scales and slime.

River-caught fish are a bit tougher to deal with, usually requiring a knife or scaling tool to rid the slab of scales. A series of bottle caps nailed to a chunk of 2x4 are the best we've found when it comes to scaling river-caught salmon, as the serrated edges swiftly lift and shuck the scales. Giving the scaled fish a rinse with the hose, to remove excess slime, is essential to further prevent strong odors from incidentally being transferred to the meat.

*Bottle caps nailed to a board is another effective means by which to remove scales and undesired slime.*

# Filleting Your Catch

There are several ways to fillet a fish, and which method you use comes down to experience and how much time you have to devote to the task. Personally, there are two basic fillet methods we like, one being quick and easy, the other requiring a bit more articulation of the knife. In either case, a long, flexible-bladed fillet knife is key to attaining the perfect cut, and the sharper the blade, the better the results. When processing fish, keep a steel or other sharpening tool handy, and use it frequently.

If pressed for time, two simple swipes of a knife can have a fillet removed and ready to cook. The first cut is made at the head, just behind the collar of the fish. This cut runs from the top to the back, all the way to the backbone, down to the throat, on the underside of the pectoral fin. Now, turn the knife on its side, keeping it flush to the backbone as the blade slides all the way to the tail.

As the knife moves along the length of the fish, the point of the blade will be exposed, either at the top of the back, or at the belly, depending on the angle at which you're working. To attain the most meat possible using this style of cut,

*Working from head to tail, two simple cuts can be made to remove a fillet.*

keep the blade close to the dorsal fin, without removing it. At the same time, the blade should run between the two pelvic fins located on the belly of the fish's midsection. These two fins can be removed from each fillet prior to cooking. With one fillet removed, flip the fish over and repeat the cuts on the other side.

Once the fillets have been removed, a portion of the ribs will have remained intact with the meat. Simply take the knife, slip the blade beneath the ribs, removing them with a shallow cut.

The only drawbacks to this technique are that by keeping the blade tight to the spine, it leaves a bit of meat on the bone, near the curve of the backbone while simultaneously removing a cartilaginous layer of backbone with the meat. If left on the meat, this layer of white tissue will dissolve and cook out, adding a milky,

*Remove any remaining rib bones and body cavity tissue.*

fatty appearance to the surface of the finished product. However, once the fillets have been removed, the long section of white tissue can be disarticulated.

To optimize the amount of meat on a fillet without having to remove the ribs or the severed edges of backbone with separate cuts, this is the approach we prefer. This technique may require a bit of practice, but removes all the meat from the bone. Holding the tail of the fish in one hand, run the tip of the blade beneath the skin, on one side of the backbone, all the way to the head. Repeat the same, lengthwise cut on the other side, leaving the dorsal fin on the carcass. Two long cuts now run the length of the backbone, from head to tail.

As in the first method, cut behind the collar of the fish from the spine to the throat, leaving the pectoral fins attached to the carcass. In both filleting methods, you may elect to keep the collar attached to the fillet, meaning the cuts will start further forward, beneath the gill plate. Like the belly, the collars have a high oil content, something you may or may not desire.

With the cuts made along the back and behind the head, work the knife from the back of the fish, down to the belly. This is where a flexible blade comes in handy, as it allows you to stay tight to the bone, working along the curves. While lifting the fillet with the opposite hand, it's easy to see where you're cutting, as

*Cutting along both sides of the backbone, and behind the gill plate to the stomach, is another way to fillet a fish.*

*Work the fillet off from back to belly. With a sharp knife, this cut can be done quickly, removing all the meat from the bone.*

opposed to cutting blindly as in the first technique described.

Work the blade down the backbone, tight against the center of the spinal column. Slide the blade over-top the spinal column, back down against the ribs as you descend to the stomach. The ribs can be removed while making this cut, which extends all the way to the middle of the belly, keeping the belly meat intact. Again, once the fillets are free, the pelvic fins can be removed.

No matter how you choose to fillet your fish, chances are, prior to being cooked or stored in the freezer, they will be handled repeatedly. To prevent damaging the soft meat through excessive handling, make two one-inch-long slits

*Making a slit at the base of each fillet makes for clean handling and results in less damage to the meat.*

through the skin near the base of the tail. Where the tail section of meat separates is where you want to make the incision. This allows you to slip a finger into the slit, carrying the finished fillets without damaging the meat. It also allows you to easily stack the meat, keeping skin touching skin or meat touching meat, so foul tastes are not transferred to the flesh.

It should be noted that given the size of these fish, though you have a nice-looking fillet, it is not boneless. There is a row of thin bones, about where the lateral line runs along the skin of a fish, that are severed when making the fillet cut. In larger fish, you will likely feel and see the blade cutting through these lateral bones as you go. In smaller fish, you may not notice their presence, especially if using a sharp knife.

Once the fillets are removed, you can see the ends of the line of lateral bones protruding from the length of fish, just above the midsection. In an uncooked fish, these bones cannot be removed without damaging the meat. The bones actually turn up toward the spine, and trying to extract them from a fillet separates the thickest, most desirable cut of meat. If you're intent on removing the bone prior to eating, do so once the meat has been cooked. At this time, the tips of bones still project from the meat and can easily be removed by hand.

We prefer leaving the skin on most of our fillets, as it helps protect the meat when freezing and in many cooking approaches. However, some people do not like the taste of fish that has been stored or cooked with the skin on, reasoning that the skin imparts a strong flavor. If desiring to remove the entire skin from a fish, this can be challenging when working with a slippery fillet. A trick is to take the fillet, place it skin side down on a cutting board, then work the blade under the tail portion of the meat. With the blade slid a quarter-inch or so between the meat and skin, dip your fingertips of the hand holding the skin into some salt. The salted fingertips provide resistance, allowing you to more easily hold the skin and slide the knife along the fillet, removing the meat from the skin in one simple cut. Keep your knife blade pressed into the skin, as if you are trying to slice the top layer of the cutting surface off. Although it may feel like you are cutting into the skin, cut firmly and keep the knife as flat as possible. You're now left with a pure meat fillet.

*No whole salmon or steelhead fillet is truly boneless, as the lateral bones remain imbedded in the upper half of the fillet.*

*Removing the lateral bones with pliers results in severe meat separation, which is fine for some recipes. To minimize tissue damage, it's best to remove these bones once the fish is cooked, as they easily slide out.*

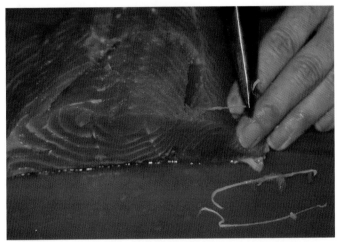

*If a skinless fillet is your desire, salting the fingers and pinning the skin to a cutting board makes for easier removal.*

# Steaking Strategies

When it comes to steaking a fish, there are only so many ways it can be done. Some people like steaking fish for the presentation it offers. Others are not too fond of it due to the high number of bones left in the cut. The thickness of the steak is determined by how much meat you wish to attain per serving, and how long you want to cook it.

When preparing a fish for steaking, cut on both sides of the head, from the top of the backbone to the belly. Be careful not to cut too deep, so as to sever the entrails where they connect to the head. You may wish to leave the collar attached, meaning the cut will start on the underside of the gill plate. The next cut runs from the anus to the throat, meeting the bottom of the first cut made.

*When preparing a fish to be cut into steaks, the head and entrails can be simultaneously removed.*

*Slit the kidney down the center and fully scrape out the remains.*

*With a finger or knife blade, force all blood out of any vessels.*

Poking a thumb and forefinger deeply into the eye sockets of the fish, apply pressure toward the belly, breaking the spine. Once the head is free, continue pulling until all the entrails are removed. This allows the head and internal organs to be removed in one piece, something that's quick, easy and comes in handy when storing for crab bait.

With the entrails gone, make a single cut down the center of the kidney, the long, dark purple organ tucked against the spine of a fish. With the butt of the knife–the fish-cleaning knives with a spoon on the end work great for this– scrape all of the kidney from the spine. If any blood remains in the veins of the fish, it can now be forced out.

Remove as much kidney from the backbone as possible, without breaking the bones. This can be done with a toothbrush.

With proper care and handling, a nice, blood-free steak is the end result.

Thoroughly rinse all blood and kidney remnants from the fish. Sometimes this can be done with a high-pressure hose. If some kidney remains in the spine sockets, use a stiff bristled toothbrush to remove it. Whatever you do, avoid using excessive force that may break the spine when attempting to free remnant kidney parts. This will result in the meat being exposed to the kidney, which will foul the taste of the final product.

With the fish clean, use a sharp knife to cut the steaks to desired width. The thinner the steaks, the more difficult they are to cut without damaging the meat. If cutting through bone is a challenge, an electric knife is excellent for steaking. When it comes to attaining a nice-looking steak, a sharp knife is prudent for slicing through the backbone and ribs. A sharp knife will cut right through the bone, while a dull blade may require hitting the joints to avoid damaging the flesh.

# Choosing a Market Fish

Not everyone who enjoys eating salmon and steelhead has the good fortune of catching them on a regular basis. While a trip to the river or ocean may find anglers heading home with a cooler full of meat once or twice a year, they may choose to further supplement their diet with store-bought fish. There are several avid fish-eaters out there who never wet a line, depending on the local market to supply them with the delightful catch.

When purchasing meat from the market, there are a few things to look for. Consumers should ask to smell and touch the fish they are considering buying. Smell is the best way to tell if a fish is bad; as the foul, amonia-like odors of deteriorating flesh are easy to detect. Usually the meat managers catch this before the consumers, but not always.

Color is another feature worth considering. The longer a fish sits, the more moisture leeches from the flesh, resulting in a pale color. Look for a clear, colorful meat with no tinges of milkiness.

Once it has passed the odor and color test, ask to touch the fish, checking it for firmness. Meat-counter attendants will typically supply you with a rubber glove with which to test the fish. Gently press the flesh, verifying there's no separation of the meat, or a tendency for it to mash together.

Another factor to consider is meat separation. Though this will have negligible impact on the overall flavor of the fish, it does indicate that a fish may have been handled by the tail, rather than by the head. Fish that has been picked up, bent, and moved about by the tail, may not only reveal meat separation, but may indicate further internal bruising, something to keep in mind when searching for a quality fillet.

How fresh a market-bought fish is depends on where the fish came from and how long it's been kept on ice. Markets specializing in handling fish – that buy them directly from commercial anglers – offer the greatest consistency when it comes to freshness. These places know the handling process intimately; that is when the fish was caught, packed in ice and delivered to their doorstep. Fish that are properly taken care of like this can be kept fresh for up to a week.

Be it a meat or seafood market, or a supermarket, look to see that the fish are kept on ice, either in fillets or whole. Whole fish placed in ice on their back, with the body cavity filled with flaked ice, is what's known as a European display. Fish displayed in this manner, with the ice regularly changed out for fresh, will keep up to four days.

When buying steelhead, there's no farmed fish that comes close to matching the flavor of a wild fish. But then again, if you don't have access to a wild steelhead, there's little alternative.

As for salmon, obtaining fresh fish can be a seasonal affair. This depends on what fishing seasons are open for what species, and can vary from region to region. Once the commercial salmon seasons have closed, no matter where you buy your fish, it's typically going to be frozen. When it comes to selecting frozen fish, wild fish is usually preferred over farmed, and in fact, a majority of people opt for frozen wild fish over fresh farmed salmon. However, like so many aspects addressed in this book, the final decision comes down to personal preference.

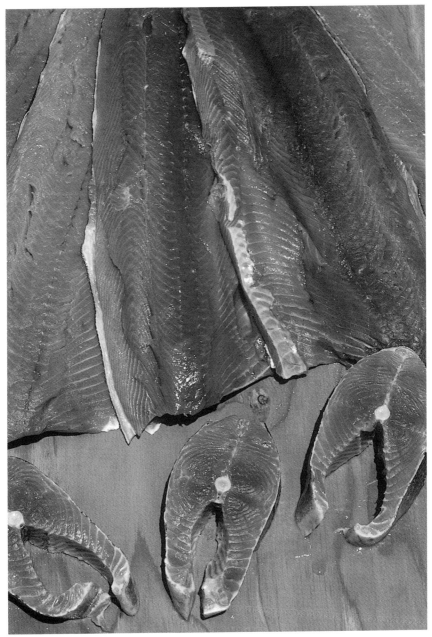

*When selecting a market fish, test its freshness by checking the color, smell and texture.*

# Freezing Uncooked Fish

T o produce the best-tasting, most nutritious fish, it's ideal to cook it fresh. But oftentimes this is unfeasible, as large quantities of fish may be caught, or the ingredients needed for a particular recipe may not be on hand. For whatever reason, freezing a raw fish is often inevitable, and contrary to many beliefs, if frozen properly, you don't have to sacrifice meat flavor or value if frozen. We regularly have a dozen or more fish in our freezer, and are happy with the end results of the fish we eat. Few people who eat this fish can detect that it's been frozen.

*Being prepared to handle high numbers of fish is critical to ensuring proper preservation.*

Fish is delicate, both in texture and flavor, and preventing air from reaching the frozen flesh, as well as water from escaping, is the objective. When exposed to air, meat loses moisture whereby the texture, color and even flavor quality is sacrificed. This is known as oxidation, which promotes freezer burn.

When freezing fish, there are certain steps that can be taken to maximize the quality of meat. Fish meat has no connective tissues, meaning as water freezes and expands in the flesh, it damages the meat. With fish, the more quickly the meat can be frozen, the better its eating quality will be. The best method is flash freezing a fish at an extremely low temperature before storing in a home freezer.

But it's unrealistic for most of us to take our fish to a meat market or butcher shop for flash freezing. So what can we do to best preserve the meat in our home freezers?

When answering this question, all that must be kept in mind is that the quicker it can be frozen, the better tasting the meat will be. Quickly freezing fillets, or better yet, parts of fillets, is the goal. By cutting fillets into meal-size portions, the smaller-size cuts freeze more rapidly. If wanting to freeze a whole fish, it's best to freeze the fillets, rather than the entire fish which takes too long to set up, resulting in mushy, pale meat once cooked.

As with fillets, if it's steaks you want, they should be cut from the fish prior to freezing. The thinner the meat, the quicker it will freeze and the higher the quality of the end product.

Ideally, fish should be frozen after the process of rigor mortis is complete and the muscle of the fish is relaxed. If placing a fish on ice immediately after catching it, the rigor stage will be more subtle, and take longer to achieve. However, on hot days, failure to place a fish on ice immediately after catching it will see it going through a harsh stage of rigor, which may cause flesh damage. Once caught, it's best to keep the fish as cool as possible, and to freeze it once it's been butchered.

The flavor of your salmon is dependent on how you have handled it from the time it's caught to the time it goes into the freezer. The meat quality will be only as good as it was when you froze it. If a fish is improperly handled and cared for prior to freezing, oxidation of fats can begin; not even freezing can stop this chemical change. This will create a very undesirable flavor and color change. To help prevent this, carry the fish by the head, not the tail, and take measures to remove all blood prior to freezing. When butchering, routinely wash the knife and handle the meat with utmost care, keeping on a clean surface at all times.

After six to eight weeks in the freezer, the flavor of the meat should be excellent, though slight toughness may be detected. To attain optimum value, fish should be consumed within the first three months of being placed in the freezer,

*However you decide to freeze your fish, the key is getting it clean and into the freezer in a timely manner.*

not for safety reasons, but because the quality of meat declines after this time period. Then again, there are ways to extend its shelf life in the freezer.

When storing meat in the freezer, vacuum sealing is regarded as the best way to go. Using our commercial sealer, we've kept fish this way for up to a year in the freezer. This technique removes as much air from the package as possible, which is the most important step when freezing fish. When thawing these packages, it's vital to remove the meat as soon as it's thawed, as mold quickly forms in this medium, even when thawed in the refrigerator. Note, vacuum sealing does not preserve fish, it only removes the air from around it. It's vital to place sealed packages in the freezer as quickly as possible.

If a food sealer is not accessible, an alternative is placing the meat in sealable baggies, whereby forcing the air out by placing it in water. With only a tiny portion of the baggy left open, submerge the baggy in a sink full of cold water, bottom end first. As the water pushes against the fish, it forces air out the top of the bag. Once to the top, close the bag when the air has been removed, making certain no water enters the bag. Wrapping this in a layer of freezer paper will allow the meat to be kept frozen for extended periods.

If you know the frozen fish will be consumed within a few months of storing, wrap the fillet in two layers of freezer paper, or other containers designed for freezing. Canning jars, plastic containers and plastic wrap made especially for the freezer are all good options. While the specialized freezer plastic wrap is more costly than the standard wrap, it's best for preserving fish. First wrapping the fish in plastic wrap, then in a layer of freezer paper is good for keeping air out, further protecting against freezer burn. You can also double wrap small fillets or steaks in the plastic wrap, then place in freezer-grade sealable bags for added protection.

Prior to placing fish in the freezer, be sure to properly label each package. Include the date caught, species, location it came from, and what cuts are inside. We even like indicating the condition of the fish, noting how it may best be prepared for consumption. You may also find it handy to note the total weight, or how many servings are in each package.

Keep in mind home freezers are not designed for rapid freezing. Avoid stacking fish on top of one another, as the resulting slow setup time fosters bacterial growth and enzymatic spoilage. The faster your salmon freezes, the less cell destruction you will have, the better the overall meat quality will be. Once frozen solid, we like stacking our fish for easy identification and to keep close track of what's in the freezer.

It's best to work fast when placing fillets inside the freezer. The longer one stands with the door open, the more cool air is being removed from the unit, the longer it will take for the fillets to freeze. Some units have areas that freeze faster than others, usually near the freezing coils, floor or walls. This is where you'll want to place your fish. Avoid placing fish inside the door of the freezer, as this takes the longest to set up and is not an optimal spot for long-term storage.

Another freezing alternative is one that's been around for years, called glazing. One of Scott's grandfathers liked freezing fish this way, and if you have time, it works well. Begin by freezing an unwrapped fish, either alone or in a plastic bag. Once frozen, dip fish, be it fillets, steaks, even small whole fish, in water and return to freezer. Repeat the process five or six more times then wrap for storage. The glazing stages may need to be repeated every six weeks, depending on how well it keeps in your freezer. Though it's a time-consuming task, it does keep the fish surface protected from oxidation.

When preparing to eat fish that has been frozen, there are a couple options. Small fillets like steelhead, small salmon, or pieces of fillet need not be thawed prior to cooking; they can be cooked while frozen by simply doubling the suggested cooking time. Since cooking frozen fish is not always possible, when thawing any fish, do so slowly by placing in the refrigerator. Note that for large fish, the thawing may take two or more days. A slow thawing process is crucial, at it reduces drip loss, where excess moisture exits the fish, decreasing its nutritional value and creating an undesirable texture. Slowly thawing a fish also protects against the growth of surface bacteria. Once a fish has been thawed, it should never be refrozen.

*Placing a fish on ice as soon as it's been caught dramatically increases the quality of its meat.*

*Vacuum packing fillets is the best way to achieve preservation in the freezer.*

# Freezing Ready-To-Cook Fish

I t was previously mentioned that we marinade or use a rub on many of our fillets prior to placing them in the freezer. Freezing stuffed fish is also an option. This is a great way to have fish ready to cook, and also means they don't need to be fully thawed in order to prepare for cooking.

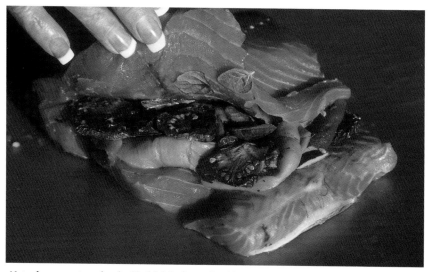

*Not only can marinated and rubbed fish be frozen, but fillets can also be stuffed and placed in the freezer.*

When we cook fish from the freezer, it's often done while the fillets are frozen solid or only partially thawed. This works best on thin fillets or sections of fillets, ones that cook evenly throughout without the edges being burnt prior to the middle being done. A general rule when cooking frozen fish is to double the cooking time recommended.

When fish completely thaws, excessive amounts of water remain in the tissues, resulting in soft, less flavorful meat that's often pale in color. Placing a frozen or partially frozen fillet on the cooking surface sees the moisture in the fish being quickly removed through intense heating and evaporation. The result is a firm, colorful fillet that many people cannot distinguish from a freshly caught fish.

However, it's not always necessary or practical to cook a frozen, marinated or rubbed fillet. For instance, when our family goes camping, we like taking fish along to eat. Often these fillets thaw prior to being cooked, but because they sit in the flavorings while thawing, their taste value does not seem to be devalued.

When it comes to storing a large number of fillets already in marinade or a rub, the real challenge is having a variety of ingredients on hand to complete an array of recipes. If days are spent on the water, it's not uncommon to have a dozen or more fish to tend when getting home. Through trial and error, we've learned that it's better to be optimistic.

*When removed from the freezer, fish can be placed directly on the grill.*

In other words, if fish are in the river and the bite's hot, or if we're going to the ocean for a slam-dunk limit of silvers, we have all the ingredients ready ahead of time. When arriving home with cleaned fillets, simply mix the ingredients for the marinades or rubs you want, spread them on the fillets, wrap and place in the freezer.

Be sure to label each fillet with the name of the marinade or rub, so it can easily be identified when it comes cooking time. It's also a good idea to label the package with the kind of fish, where it came from and when it was caught. These steps will help keep the rotation of fillets up to date, so as to prevent freezer damage by having them remain in the freezer too long. If using a permanent marker, write this information on a label, for it may pass through some grades of freezer paper and come in contact with the meat.

Mind you, not all fillets need be marinated, rubbed or stuffed prior to freezing because you may be preparing them in different ways, or unsure of the recipe you want to use at the time of freezing. In this case, remove the fish from the freezer, and if the recipe allows, start cooking it immediately, adding the ingredients as you go. As a last resort, fillets can be fully thawed prior to cooking, but again, do so slowly in the refrigerator. Avoid thawing at room temperature, or worse yet, by placing in water as this will accentuate rapid drip loss, resulting in soft, drab-tasting meat.

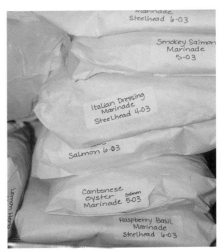

A few days after freezing fillets, we like stacking them atop one another, on the same shelf so we can keep track of what's in the freezer, and quickly and easily read each label. When adding new fish to the freezer, the already frozen ones work great to quickly cool the new additions.

*Once frozen, fillets can be stacked in the freezer to better keep track of what's on hand.*

# Canning Fish

Canning fish is one of the best ways to ensure long-term preservation. But for younger generations who may not have been raised in households where canning was part of the lifestyle, conquering this technique can be difficult, even intimidating. That's why we called upon Master Food Preserver, Sharon Weber, for assistance on this topic. Sharon is a volunteer with the Oregon State University Lane County Extension service, specializing in food preservation.

When preserving any food, safety is the number one-concern. Your local extension office can be a wealth of information and most have volunteers that can help you access their resources for any questions you may have that are not answered here. They may also have free classes you can take to learn the entire canning process in a hands-on setting.

If using a dial-gauge pressure canner, it is imperative to have the gauge checked for accuracy once a year. Some extension offices will do this free of charge, or for a minimal cost. Check your gasket and replace it if there is any question as to its condition. Be sure to follow the manufacturer's owners manual processing procedures for your canner. If you no longer have the directions, contact the manufacturer and get them. Two very important points: Follow the directions in your book for the amount of cool water specified and always vent the canner. This is not to be guess work.

You must use a 16 or 22-quart pressure canner for canning salmon and steelhead. There are no tested processing times for smaller pressure canners or quart jars. It is never safe to reduce processing times when you are canning.

Before starting the canning process, make sure the fish is of good quality. Do not use any fish that is questionable. Apply the following steps:

**Step 1:** Bleed and gut fish right after catching it. It is best to chill it as quickly as possible, until you are ready to can.

**Step 2:** Fillet and split fish lengthwise. Cut into similar-sized pieces suitable for the canning jar.

**Step 3:** Pack fish tightly into either pint or half-pint jars. The size jar you use depends on the amount of fish you intend on eating each time a jar is opened. It is optional to add 1 teaspoon salt per pint. Leave 1" headspace in the jar. There is no need to add liquid.

**Step 4:** Moisten a paper towel with vinegar and wipe the jar rims clean. This is helpful anytime you are canning fatty fish, as it will help achieve a good seal. Place lid on jar and screw on the band. Process half-pints and pints for 100 minutes. The pressure depends on your elevation, and also whether you are using a weighted-gauge canner or a dial-gauge.

DIAL-GAUGE PRESSURES

- Sea level to 2,000 feet elevation, use 11 pounds pressure.
- 2,001 to 4,000 feet elevation, use 12 pounds pressure.

- 4,001 to 6,000 feet elevation, use 13 pounds pressure.
- 6,001 to 8,000 feet elevation, use 14 pounds pressure.

WEIGHTED-GAUGE CANNER:
- Sea level to 1,000 feet elevation, use a 10-pound weight.
- Over 1,000 feet elevation, use a 15-pound weight.

**Step 5:** Remove the canner from the heat after it has been processed for the appropriate amount of time. Let the pressure return to zero before opening the canner. DO NOT try to get the pressure to drop quicker than it does on its own. All processing times figure-in getting up to temperature and cool down time.

**Step 6:** Remove the jars from the canner and let cool.

**Step 7:** Test your jars in 24 hours to ensure there is a good seal. If you have only one or two that didn't seal, you can put those in the refrigerator to consume right away, or freeze them. If you have many jars that didn't seal, remove the old lid and ring, put on a new lid, tighten the screw ring down and reprocess in the canner. You must reprocess these again for the entire length of time. If you choose to freeze what didn't seal, make certain you remove the screw band, let it freeze, then put the screw band back on. This will keep the jar from exploding.

**Step 8:** Label and date the jars accordingly.

Constant monitoring is necessary during processing. This is not a time to put the pressure canner on the stove and go on to other projects. For dial-gauges, be sure to periodically check to make sure it is maintaining the proper pressure. Weighted-gauges are also easy to manage, as you can listen to them. They should jiggle or rock a specified number of times per minute, as indicated in the directions for your canner. Once you get used to the rhythm, you'll know when it is rocking properly.

SAFETY TIPS

Before opening any home-canned fish, check for spoilage. There are many signs. If the lid is bulging before removing it, if the liquid spurts out, if it smells odd, or any mold is present, it is NOT safe to eat. Do not taste anything that is questionable; botulism is odorless, colorless and tasteless. You must depend on safe and proper canning methods when canning your salmon.

After opening a jar of salmon, be sure to wash the lid off, even if you are

*Canning is the best long-term storage option for fish.*

going to throw it away. It's especially important to thoroughly wash the lid if you plan on reusing it on the opened jar.

As an added safety measure, it's best to heat home-canned fish before eating it. To destroy any toxin that may have formed, boil the fish for 10 minutes on the stovetop. You may also achieve this by heating it in the oven, while in the jar you canned it in. Use a meat thermometer with the tip in the center of the jar. Cover the jar with foil and place it in a preheated oven at 350°F. It will take approximately 30-35 minutes for the thermometer to register 185°F, at which time the process is complete.

When canning fish, questions may arise. One of the more common relates to the glass-like crystals that have formed in the canned salmon. Which is magnesium ammonium phosphate and usually dissolves once you heat the fish. They are not harmful to your health. You did nothing wrong that caused the crystals to form, and there is no way to prevent their formation.

Another commonly asked question, is why didn't the jars seal. Believe it or not, lids can get old just sitting around in the cupboard, unused. Always use new, fresh lids.

By adhering to the information shared here, the owner's manual that came with your cooker, and perhaps your local extension office, you will be ready to go when it comes time to can your own salmon and steelhead. Not only will the act of canning be rewarding, but preserving fish in this way makes for convenient, enjoyable meals.

*Using fresh lids is critical to attaining a perfect seal.*

# Cooking Tips

How do you really judge when a fish is done cooking? This is a basic, yet complicated topic deserving attention, for one of the most common errors made is overcooking fish. The first thing to keep in mind is that if a salmon or steelhead is freshly caught it can be served quite rare with pleasing results. If however a fish has been purchased at the market or has been previously frozen, people may feel more comfortable if it is fully cooked.

Fish is considered completely cooked once its internal temperature reaches 140°. Bear in mind however, that because fish takes such little heat to cook, it continues cooking once removed from the heat source. Once the temperature of a fish exceeds 140°, its tissue begins to break down and it becomes overcooked, with a less than desirable flavor and texture. If fish breaks easily into tiny flakes, it has been overcooked.

Many restaurants cook their fish to 125° or 130° and although they may not be following food safety regulations to a T, they state that too many overcooked fish are sent back to the kitchen. We suggest cooking the fish until it is opaque and flakes in large chunks.

Cooking time varies for fresh fish, frozen fish, stuffed fish or fish cooked in parchment paper or aluminum foil. If fish is fresh, success will be had with any cooking method following the general guideline of cooking 10 minutes for every 1" of thickness.

When cooking frozen fish, baking, grilling or sealing it in parchment or aluminum foil is recommended and the cooking time needs to be doubled.

*A meat thermometer is essential for monitoring the internal temperature of cooked fish.*

Previously frozen fish, when properly thawed in the refrigerator, can be prepared using any cooking method but may require less cooking time if it was frozen in a marinade. A bit of extra oil may need to be added since some of the oils are broken down in the freezing process.

The beauty of cooking your own fish is the many ways it can be prepared. The dishes can be surprisingly simple, adding to the overall enjoyment of your home-cooked meal. By taking care not to overcook your salmon and steelhead, the end result will be one that impresses everyone, every time, including yourself.

*Taking your catch from the water to the platter is one of the greatest opportunities nature has to offer.*

# Index